POWER SISTERS

Copyright © 2023 Power Sisters- All Rights Reserved

No part of this publication may be used or reproduced in a manner without the prior permission from the author except in the case of a brief quotation embodied in articles or reviews.

For information, visit:
www.fromHeavenbooks.com

First edition Printed in the United States of America
Written by: Greg Hendry
Cover by: Ronny Kim of iAmplify
Edited by : Peter Evans, Micaela Hamilton, Linda Black, Sarah Coulter, and Glenn Hendry Jr.

CHAPTERS

	Introduction	5
1.	St. Teresa of Calcutta- Power Mother and Missionary	11
2.	St. Teresa Benedicta of the Cross (Edith Stein)- Power Jewish Convert & Martyr	23
3.	Saint Sister Mary Antona Ebo- Power Social Activist	35
4.	Mother Angelica – Power television broadcaster	47
5.	Sister Dede Byrne POSC- Power Veteran and Surgeon	63
6.	Mother Dolores Hart O.S.B.- Power Movie Star	75
7.	Sister Josephine Garrett, CSFN- Power Baptist Convert and Unruly Speaker	87
8.	Sister M. Therese Antone, RSM, Ed.D- Power University President and Chancellor	99
9.	Sister Maris Stella Karalekas- Power Naval Sister for Life	111
10.	Sister Alicia Torres F.E.- Power Runner & Chef	121
11.	Sister Madonna Buder- Power Iron Nun	131
12.	Sister Miriam James Heidland- Power Hitter, Author, and Podcaster	143
13.	Wrap Up	155

INTRODUCTION

"Spread love everywhere you go." – Saint Teresa of Calcutta

The year is 1997, and the world has lost one of the most iconic leaders of the 20th century. In a century that included two world wars, numerous inventions, and the most significant growth in corporate wealth led primarily by iconic male inventors and military, political, and business leaders, arguably none spread more of God's love around the world than a diminutive woman from Albania known then as Mother Teresa.

Reading this in the 21st century, when a push for gender equality has opened more doors for women, may diminish the irony. Still, over two thousand years prior, the foundation for great women was established by a young woman we know as Mary of Nazareth. Her obedience to God's call to be the mother of our Savior, Jesus, made her queen of heaven and earth since, traditionally, queens were the king's mother.

If the fact that the greatest purely human was a woman surprises anyone, perhaps the words of a great Catholic contemporary of Mother Teresa's said it best.

The two would both receive the designation of Saint by the Catholic Church, and Mother Teresa would forever be known as St. Teresa of Calcutta. The Catholic Church would add a poor town in India to this iconic woman's name not because it was where she was born but because it was where she shared God's love with the poorest of the poor while struggling with her faith.

"Women possess feminine genius." – Saint John Paul II

POWER SISTERS | 5

Yes, this Nobel Peace Prize winner and iconic saint did not stop loving others even while she struggled with her faith!

The other power sisters profiled represent religious women's diverse influence on education, healthcare, social justice, and the Catholic Church. Although capturing all past and current influencers is impossible, these imperfect women represent a cross-section of orders who have answered their vocational call and changed the world in service to God.

Religious sisters have founded schools, hospitals, monasteries, and religious orders to support many Catholics along their journey to develop a strong mind, body, and soul. Our healthcare and educational systems would not be the same without their influence.

Appropriately, in the year that Pope Francis gave women the unprecedented right to vote at a meeting of bishops, *Power Sisters* recognizes the contributions religious sisters have made and continue to make. With four deceased sisters profiled along with eight living, the hope is to bridge the influencers of the past with those of the present as women gain greater decision-making responsibilities within the Catholic Church.

All Christians can draw wisdom and strength from these women and Mary, our mother in heaven. The specifics on new voting rights for the synod include:

- Five religious sisters join five priests as voting representatives for religious orders
- Women make up half of the seventy non-bishop voting members

Before diving into these amazing stories, it is worth briefly clarifying the history and role of religious sisters. The consecrated life has been part of religion even before the time of Christ. Since many of Christ's disciples were women, the role continued in the Church He established, evolving over the centuries.

Transcending the established norms of His time, Jesus treated women with openness, respect, acceptance, and tenderness. In this way, He honored the dignity women have always possessed according to God's plan.

At Christ's crucifixion, some of those women showed that their gender had the power and hearts to carry on His message of love and mercy. While His apostle and first Pope was denying Him three times, three women accompanied his mother at the foot of the cross.

> *"Standing by the cross of Jesus were his mother, his mother's sister, Mary the wife of Clopas, and Mary Magdalene"*
> –John 19:25

The twelve religious sisters featured represent the women past, present, and future who, by the grace of the Holy Spirit, have made and will make a powerful impact on many. Along their journey to bring Christ to the world, they have served the poorest of the poor and shown Gold's love and mercy to many.

As background, both nuns and sisters are typically addressed as Sisters, but there are some differences. Nuns' lives are generally spent in prayer and work within their convent or monastery, while Sisters are more active in the world, engaging in many kinds of work. Some of these power sisters blur those lines, but all have made vows to serve faithfully.

Although no single book can summarize the outstanding achievements of all Catholic sisters over the years, this author humbly prays that these stories may inspire more in the future and shares with gratitude.

Oh, The Love and Mercy a Sister Shall Bestow

Oh, the love and mercy you shall bestow!
There is much to be done!
There are souls to be saved and hearts to be won.
And the amazing things you can do with God's
call, will help bring His loving message to all.

Amen! You'll be as powerful as a woman can be,
With many followers online, in the classroom, or on TV.
You have brains in your head. You have feet in your shoes.
God can steer you in any direction He
or your Mother superior may choose.
And when you're guiding young sheep as a teacher, nurse, or nun
You'll pray often to God and perhaps suffer some like his Son.

You were pioneers in the fields of education and healthcare.
Spreading the message of God to students everywhere
While opening the first hospitals for everyone's health
Doing it all for love, not for your personal wealth

Today is the Lord's day!
His people are waiting.
So please get on your way!
Out there, things can happen and frequently do,
To people as trained and holy as you.
Don't fear when bad things happen
since God will get you through.
Just lean on your faith, and His glory will shine true!

Your mission is to show God's mercy.
The real example of power to all those in need

Following Mary's example of obedience and love
Using your feminine genius to plant that seed.

After your journey in this life
By God's grace, you will be old
May you come to a place where the streets are of gold,
And the holy choir of angels will be much to behold.

With the Father, Son, and Holy Spirit
His followers in heaven will be as one.
Thanks to a caring Sister, they learned,
Through Jesus and the cross, the battle was won.

Greg Hendry 2023

CHAPTER 1

SAINT TERESA OF CALCUTTA
POWER MOTHER AND MISSIONARY

"Spread love everywhere you go."
"Not all of us can do great things, but we can do small things with great love." –St. Teresa

The incredible St. Teresa of Calcutta, more commonly known as Mother Teresa, is the subject of many books and a few movies. Yet before her death, very few knew about her long-term inner struggles with her faith. The focus of this chapter will include not only her amazing work after her call within a call that made her a saint but also those struggles that she grew to embrace.

Mother Teresa shared her internal struggles with her faith in her private letters to her spiritual advisors. Still, these writings were kept private until Mother Teresa: *Come Be My Light* was published 22 years after her death.

The book is a moving chronicle of St. Teresa's spiritual journey from a young girl in love with her faith, accepting God's call to missionary work in India, and later founding an order dedicated to helping the poorest of the poor. The journey included over a decade of utter desolation and emptiness in her faith, during which her interior life was marked by a deep, painful, and abiding feeling of being separated from God. She felt rejected by Him while she longed for His love. She called her inner experience the darkness.

> *"If I ever become a Saint, I will surely be one of darkness. I will continually be absent from Heaven to light the light of those in darkness on earth."*
> – Mother Teresa

Despite these interior struggles, Mother Teresa provided a life of service to the poorest of the poor and became an icon of compassion to people of all religions. Her extraordinary contributions to the care of the sick and the dying were acclaimed worldwide. Through the darkness, she mystically participated in the thirst of Jesus, which she defined as His painful and burning longing for love, and she sought to satisfy His thirst by sharing in the interior desolation of the poor and serving their needs.

The painful night of her soul, which began when she started her work for the poor and continued to the end of her life, led her to an ever more profound union with God.

Through these trials, Saint Teresa emerges with the fire of charity since her heart was not only tested but purified by this long and intense trial of faith. Her internal suffering did not diminish her faith but ultimately drew her closer to Jesus.

What can these struggles teach us when our faith is sterile, or we are in our own darkness? Do we reject our Catholic faith when we experience difficulties, or do we embrace them as a means of unification with Christ's sufferings, bringing us closer to God?

> *"I have grown to love the darkness"* – Mother Teresa

> *"Give Jesus a big smile each time you feel your nothingness. Keep giving Jesus to others, not by words, but by your example of being in love with Jesus. Keep the joy of Jesus as your strength."* – Mother Teresa

The remarkable woman who would be known as Mother Teresa began life named Gonxha Agnes Bojaxhiu. She was born on August 26, 1910, in the city of Skopje, now in Northern Macedonia.

She was the youngest child of three born to her Catholic Albanian parents, Nikola and Drane Bojaxhiu. She received her First Communion at age five and was confirmed in November 1916. Her father died when she was only nine, leaving her family in financial straits.

Her faith-filled mother was her first teacher, and her religious formation was assisted by the vibrant Jesuit parish of the Sacred Heart, in which she was very involved as a youth. Inspired by the Jesuits and their history as missionaries, Mother Teresa had her first sense of a religious vocation at age twelve. During her teenage years, she voraciously read stories about the Jesuit missions, particularly in Bengal, India.

Moved to pursue missionary work, Gonxha left her home in September 1928 at the age of eighteen to join the Institute of the Blessed Virgin Mary, known as the Sisters of Loreto, in Ireland. One year later, she received the name Sister Mary Teresa after St. Therese of Lisieux and departed for her first trip to India, arriving in Calcutta. After making her First Profession of Vows in May 1931, Sister Teresa was assigned to the Loreto Entally community in Calcutta and taught at St. Mary's School for girls.

Six years later, Sister Teresa made her Final Profession of Vows. She continued teaching at St. Mary's School, and in 1944, at age 34, she became the school's principal.

POWER SISTERS | 13

Her natural talent for organization and capacity for hard work fit well into her role as principal, but God had other plans for her. Her twenty years in Loreto were filled with profound happiness, but she could not ignore the call within the call.

> *"Whatever you did for one of these least of my brothers, you did for me."*
> –Matthew 25:40

While Mother Teresa was serving as a school principal in Loreta, the country of India was suffering. During the great famine of Bengal in 1943, an estimated 3 million people perished from starvation, malaria, and other diseases aggravated by malnutrition, population displacement, unsanitary conditions, and lack of health care. A combination of factors, including government policies, wartime disruption of food distribution, and an unusually high cyclone and flood, contributed to the travesties.

Another source of suffering in the country then was violent disputes between Muslims and Hindus, which were so severe that the Muslim League took direct action toward a separate Muslim homeland after the British exit from India. The large-scale violence between Muslims and Hindus in Calcutta led to the death of as many as 5,000 men on August 16, 1946.

> *"Love cannot remain by itself – it has no meaning. Love must be put into action, and that action is service."* –Mother Teresa

Less than a month later, on September 10, 1946, during a train ride from Calcutta to Darjeeling for her annual retreat, Mother Teresa received her inspiration, her "call within a call." On that day, in a way she could never fully explain, Jesus' thirst for love and souls took hold of her heart, and the desire to satiate His thirst became the driving force of her life.

She heard God tell her, "You will have to go to the slums and serve the poorest of the poor." Jesus revealed to her the desire of His heart: "He begged her. 'I cannot go alone. Come be My light.'"

Jesus revealed His pain at the neglect of the poor, His sorrow at their ignorance of Him, and His longing for their love. He asked Mother Teresa to establish a religious community, Missionaries of Charity, dedicated to serving the poorest of the poor.

Nearly two years of asking and discernment passed before Mother Teresa received permission from her bishop to begin her own order. On August 17, 1948, she dressed for the first time in a white, blue-bordered sari (a simple, traditional Indian garment) and passed through the gates of her beloved Loreto convent to enter the world of the neediest.

After a short course with the Medical Mission Sisters in Patna, Mother Teresa returned to Calcutta and found temporary lodging with the Little Sisters of the Poor. On December 21, she went for the first time to the slums. She visited families, washed children's sores, cared for an older man lying sick on the road, and nursed a woman dying of hunger and tuberculosis. She started each day with communion, then went out, rosary in her hand, to find and serve Him among the unwanted, the unloved, the abandoned. After some months, she was joined by twelve of her former students.

Four years after hearing the call, Mother Teresa became an official citizen of India, and the Archdiocese of Calcutta established the Missionaries of Charity. Their mission was to satiate the thirst of Jesus because when He was dying on the cross, He said, "I thirst." According to Mother Teresa's understanding, Jesus never asked for water. He asked for souls to love him and to satisfy his commandment to serve the needs of others.

In the 1950s, the Sisters of Charity worked primarily with the destitute in Calcutta, where they attended to the sick, the dying, and the leprous. On top of that, they reached out to the city's many homeless children, giving them shelter and love. The home she opened, Nirmala Shishu Bhavan, welcomed any child who arrived there.

By the early 1960s, Mother Teresa began to send her sisters to other parts of India, and to respond better to both the physical and spiritual needs of the poor, Mother Teresa founded the Missionaries of Charity Brothers in 1963.

The Decree of Praise granted to the Congregation by Pope Paul VI in February 1965 encouraged her to open a house in Venezuela. It was soon followed by foundations in Rome and Tanzania and, eventually, on every continent. She started homes for people with leprosy and provided jobs for them, including making the sisters' saris.

During these years of rapid growth for the order in the 1960s and 70s, the world began to turn its eyes towards Mother Teresa and the work she had started. Numerous awards, beginning with the Indian Padmashri Award in 1962 and notably the Nobel Peace Prize in 1979, honored her work. She received both prizes humbly for the glory of God and in the name of the poor.

In her speeches after receiving each award, she focused on three themes:

1. **Forgotten elderly-** "Loneliness and the feeling of being unwanted is the most terrible poverty."
2. **Neglected children-** "How can there be too many children? That is like saying there are too many flowers?"
3. **Unborn children-** "Any country that accepts abortion is not teaching its people to love but to use violence to get what they want."

Even as world leaders were honored to meet her, Mother Teresa longed for a light in her personal dark relationship with God.

In her letters to the various Bishops who served as her spiritual directors, she often talked about her loneliness while traveling around the world receiving awards.

She mentioned her deep, painful, and abiding feeling of being separated from God, even rejected by Him, along with an ever-increasing longing for His love. She called her inner experience the "painful night" of her soul.

> "Suffering is a sign you are so close to Jesus. So close He can kiss you." –Mother Teresa

POWER SISTERS | 17

She eventually grew to love the darkness as a shared suffering with Jesus' thirst for souls and His longing for our love and shared empathy with the poorest of the poor. This love for the darkness and the advice of Pope Paul to "listen to Jesus" propelled the global expansion of the Sisters of Charity.

> *"If there are poor on the moon, I would go there too."*
> – Mother Teresa

In the 1980s and early '90s, Mother Teresa opened houses in almost all the communist countries, including the former Soviet Union, Albania, and Cuba, where atheism dominated. She expanded her congregation's work to support patients suffering from AIDS. In 1985, the United Nations secretary called her the most influential person in the world.

This little woman, who barely stood five feet tall and had limited formal education, had risen to power and worldwide notoriety by following two simple rules:

1. Listen to Jesus
2. Spread love wherever you go.

Mother Teresa's inspiration was not limited to those with religious vocations. She met with political leaders worldwide, including U.S. President Ronald Reagan and UK's Lady Diana, spreading her message of love. She also formed groups like the Co-Workers of Mother Teresa, which consisted of people of many faiths and nationalities who shared her spirit of prayer, simplicity, sacrifice, and love.

She respected all religions and saw Jesus in all of them. Her mission was to feed, clothe, and shelter those in need.

Despite increasingly severe health problems towards the end of her life, Mother Teresa continued to govern her Society and respond to the needs of the poor and the Church. By 1997,

Mother Teresa's Sisters numbered nearly 4,000 members and were established in 610 foundations in 123 countries.

In March 1997, she blessed her newly-elected successor as Superior General of the Missionaries of Charity and then made one more trip abroad to the United States and Rome. In the U.S., she visited the Missionaries of Charity home in New York City. She was treated by power sister Dede Byrne MD when she fell ill in Washington D.C. Both houses of the US Congress halted debates so members could attend an hour-long tribute to her at which she received the Congressional Gold Medal, the highest honor Congress can give a civilian.

After meeting Pope John Paul II in Rome, she returned to Calcutta and spent her final weeks receiving visitors and instructing her Sisters before passing away on Sep 5, 1997, at the age of 87.

St. Teresa of Calcutta was canonized by Pope Francis on September 4, 2016, in a ceremony witnessed by tens of thousands of people, including 1,500 homeless people across Italy.

POWER SISTERS | 19

She is the patron saint of World Youth Day, Missionaries of Charity, and a co-patron of the Archdiocese of Calcutta alongside St. Francis Xavier. Her feast day is celebrated on September 5th, the date of her passing from this earth.

Despite her passing over a quarter century ago, her influence remains strong. The Sisters of Charity have expanded to 139 countries, and in 2022, The Knights of Columbus sponsored a movie about her amazing life entitled *Mother Teresa: No Greater Love*. It was released in limited theaters but grossed over $1.2 million in the first weekend. The world had not forgotten this incredible woman 25 years after her passing.

> *"She was a small, tiny, bent woman with a commanding presence. You could feel an aura about her. An aura not of power, but an aura of simplicity and holiness."*
> Sunil Lucas- Filmmaker

CHAPTER CHALLENGE

FAITH CHALLENGE

- Saint Teresa of Calcutta spent an hour daily in front of the Eucharist. Consider spending some time once a week in front of the Eucharist and contemplate what God asks of you. If you are in a dark place, ask St. Teresa of Calcutta to help you find your way back so you can be a light for someone else.
- Consider watching the film *Mother Teresa: No Greater Love* or reading one of the many books about St. Teresa of Calcutta. One chapter cannot do her life of service justice.

WORKS CHALLENGE

- Find some time to serve others. Maybe start with visiting a friend who just returned home from the hospital or making a meal for a family who just welcomed a new baby? Or maybe visiting the elderly in a nursing home? Mother Teresa always encouraged us to love those around us, but perhaps you can expand the volunteering and support the poorest of the poor. Try placing everyone else's needs in front of your own for a week.

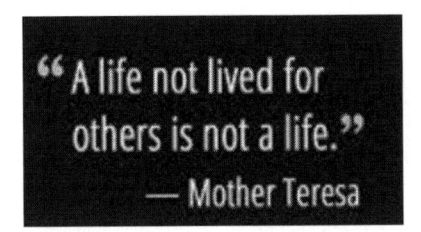

> "A life not lived for others is not a life."
> — Mother Teresa

CHAPTER 2

SAINT TERESA BENEDICTA OF THE CROSS (EDITH STEIN)

POWER JEWISH CONVERT & MARTYR

"Love conquers fear.." –Edith Stein

The woman who would become Saint Teresa Benedicta of the Cross was born Edith Stein in 1891. She was the youngest of eleven children and came into this world while her family was celebrating the Day of Atonement or Yom Kippur, the holiest day of the Jewish calendar.

She was born and raised in Breslau, Germany, which today is renamed Wroclaw, Poland. The residents were primarily German-speaking Christians, but her family was part of the small (5%) Jewish community with significant global influences.

Edith's father died when she was only two, so her mother, a woman of deep faith, raised her, emphasizing education and critical thinking. However, some of that critical thinking misled Edith to stop believing in God as a teenager, and Edith gave up praying.

While she studied at several universities toward her doctorate in philosophy, this young Jewish woman had no time for religion. She was fully absorbed with life and unconcerned with eternal life. Why look to God for answers when you can find the answers in a book? Meanwhile, two Jewish professors with ties to her home, Breslau, were impacting the world. In 1906, Alois Alzheimer gave a now-famous talk in southern Germany. He described the unusual disease of the cerebral cortex, which caused symptoms of memory loss, disorientation, and hallucinations. It wasn't until 1910 that "Alzheimer's disease" was formally named after this future chair of the Department of Psychology at the University in Breslau in the 8th edition of the *Handbook of Psychiatry*.

A few years later, another Jewish psychologist at the university in Breslau, William Stern, introduced the concept of intelligence quotient (IQ). This measurement is still used to formulate a person's reasoning and problem-solving abilities.

$$IQ = \frac{\text{mental age}}{\text{chronological age}} \times 100$$

Why introduce two Jewish male thought leaders in a book about a saint? In less than three decades, Jews across Europe, and particularly in Germany, would face atrocious discrimination and murder just because of the ludicrous notion that they were an inferior race.

Soon after these men's contributions, Europe was at war. During the war, which would become known as the First World War, Edith completed her PhD, an extremely rare accomplishment for women at that time and uncommon for men. She also worked as a nursing assistant, witnessing firsthand the horrible tragedies of combat. Although she was still an atheist, God began calling her into a life in the spirit soon after her experiences.

Edith saw a woman praying in the Frankfurt Cathedral shortly after the war. She was impressed by the piety of Christians who visited churches even when nothing special happened. She saw the widow of a dear friend who had died during the war and was amazed at the young woman's profound faith and faith-filled serenity.

Edith remarked:

"This was my first encounter with the cross and the divine power it imparts to those who bear it...it was the moment when my unbelief collapsed, and Christ began to shine His light on me—Christ the mystery of the cross."

God had opened the door to Edith's mind and heart.

A few years later, at a friend's house, Edith found a copy of the autobiography of Saint Teresa of Avila and stayed up through the night to read it. Edith knew then that she had found the truth. She was baptized only months later, on January 1, 1922. Still, the Lord had not finished her transformation.

Following her conversion in 1922, Stein immersed herself in Catholic philosophy, translating St. Thomas Aquinas's *On Truth*. Her studies and previous writings had focused primarily on phenomenology, which can be described as the study of consciousness and the objects of direct experience. This type of philosophy focuses on experience as the ultimate source of all meaning and values the lived experience of many.

While working with two giants in philosophy, Martin Heidegger and Edmund Husserl, Edith developed her critical thinking and sense of faith. Martin Heidegger was also of Jewish descent, and he and his wife also converted to Christianity.

While studying under Martin Heidegger, Edith developed her conception of God. She concluded that although our experiences can have varying degrees of emptiness and fullness, we can experience perfect fullness through God. That belief directly opposed her mentor Martin Heidegger's account of finitude, which considered human lives finite. Although a single chapter in this book could not explore the depth of these two philosophers, Edith's beliefs led her along the road to sainthood while her mentor went on to support the Nazis.

Edith's contributions did not stop with philosophy; she also wrote a report commissioned by the Ministry of Education on women's education and educational reform.

> *"When you seek truth, you seek God whether you know it or not."* –Edith Stein

While teaching philosophy, Edith's love for learning and the pursuit of truth propelled her to know and love God more. She desired to give God her mind, gifts, energy, and heart, and she felt drawn to the Carmelite order. Out of respect for her Jewish mother, whom Edith's conversion to Catholicism had deeply hurt, she delayed an immediate move to the religious life.

In 1933, when Nazi anti-Jewish laws forced her to give up her teaching position, she entered the Carmelite community as Sister Teresa Benedicta of the Cross.

> *"Each woman who lives in the light of eternity can fulfill her vocation, whether in marriage, religious order, or a worldly profession."* –Edith Stein

With the Carmelite nuns, Sister Teresa Benedicta was drawn to the life and spirituality of Thérèse of Lisieux. For those unfamiliar with this other great saint, Thérèse of Lisieux was a Carmelite nun from France who died from tuberculosis in 1897 at the tender age of 24. She has been nicknamed The Little Flower since she was so young, and on her death bed, she shared, *"When I die, I will send down a shower of roses from the heavens; I will spend my heaven doing good upon earth."*

She never left the convent after joining as a teenager and even had a problem with falling asleep during community prayer. However, her only book, *The Story of a Soul*, went viral in today's terms and is still read by many today.

Her "Little Way" emphasized simply "always doing the smallest right and doing it all for love."

> *"I understood that every flower created by Him is beautiful, that the brilliance of the rose and the whiteness of the lily do not lessen the perfume of the violet or the sweet simplicity of the daisy… And so, it is in the world of souls, our Lord's living garden."*
> – St. Thérèse of Lisieux

Edith would also do her share of small things right for love, including writing. She wrote one of the books, *Life in a Jewish Family*, to encourage the next generation of young Jewish people who were now growing up in a world of persecution, violence, and prejudice. She wanted to remind them of how wonderful life had been and could be again. She also urged the German people to see that all families were alike in many ways.

(St. Thérèse of Lisieux)

These two saints shared timeless reminders that just as flowers come in different colors and are all part of the same garden, various races, and faiths are also part of God's wonderfully created universe.

Edith's other writings focused on helping people understand the unique value of women and how they contributed to a prosperous society. For context, women in the United States didn't gain the right to vote until 1920, when the 19th Amendment was passed, and Edith was coincidentally 19 years old.

> "*The participation of women in the most diverse professional disciplines could be a blessing for the entire society.*" –Edith Stein

When Nazi leader Adolf Hitler came to power in 1938, the persecution of Jews became more systematic and open. To protect Edith, who had to wear the star of David on her habit because she came from a Jewish family, her Carmelite superior in Cologne, Germany, transferred Edith and her sister, Rosa (who had also become Catholic and was a Carmelite extern) to a monastery in Holland, to get them out of harm's way.

An extern's primary responsibilities and service of love are to take care of the exterior duties connected with the monastery, enabling the cloistered Sisters to live their vocation of hidden immolation in solitude.

Given the imminent threat to these Catholic nuns with Jewish roots, the move to Echt, Holland, seemed wise, but Edith was not afraid. She even wrote a prophetic request to God.

> "*I beg the Lord to take my life and my death...as atonement for the unbelief of the Jewish People.*"

She lived by her motto, "Love conquers fear," even while Nazis were burning synagogues and terrorizing Jews in Germany. Her main concern was that her Jewish people would come to know Jesus Christ as the savior promised to her people as outlined in the Old Testament.

Just as Jesus of Nazareth had been raised for 30 years in the traditions of the Jewish faith along with his apostles, Edith read about the prophets and stories that foretold his coming. Like Jesus, she was even willing to sacrifice her life for all to believe.

Following the 1940 Nazi invasion and occupation of the Netherlands, Edith's willingness to sacrifice her life drew closer to reality. In response to a statement by the Dutch Catholic Bishops at a conference in 1942 condemning the Nazis' persecution and deportation of Jews, the Gestapo (the Nazi secret police) raided religious communities in the Netherlands to arrest and deport any Jewish converts sheltered there.

On August 2, 1942, Edith and her sister Rosa were arrested in the convent's chapel and hauled away. As they were being taken out, Edith was overheard telling Rosa, *"Come, we are going for our people."*

After a lengthy train ride in an airless, dirty boxcar packed tightly with fellow Jews, the two sisters ended up in Auschwitz, the most feared of the thousands of concentration camps established by the Nazi party. These death camps were run by Hitler's SS troops, fanatic loyalists who embodied the Nazi party's distorted definition of racial purity.

Although their oath scandalously cites God, and even though the party witnessed African American Jesse Owens win four gold medals in the 1936 Olympics hosted in Berlin, the Nazis did not buy into the notion shared by Edith Stein and St. Therese that every flower and human created by God was beautiful.

"I vow to you, Adolf Hitler...so help me God."
Excerpt of SS Loyalty Oath

POWER SISTERS | 29

Instead of recognizing the contributions of great Jewish minds from Breslau, like Edith Stein, Alzheimer, and William Stern, these SS troops chose blind loyalty to a distorted notion that one race was superior to others instead of seeking the truth revealed by God. Appropriately, one does not need a high IQ to dismiss this notion and follow the little way.

Within a week of arriving in Auschwitz, German SS troops shoved Edith, her sister, and many of her fellow Jews into a gas chamber where Edith would get her heroic prayer answered. Edith gave up her life for the atonement of her Jewish people.

A great intellect who sought truth and spoke out against prejudice was gone, but she left an extraordinary example of a sacrificial life. Like the women who stood at the foot of the cross when Jesus was crucified for our sins, Sister Teresa Benedicta's love of God and neighbor overcame her human fear when facing death.

She was an intelligent, Catholic, solid woman of Jewish heritage who used her knowledge to help others grow in the understanding of themselves, especially women. God values and loves women, giving them many unique strengths, including the exclusive power to bring life into the world.

Although her own life was cut short, the world has not forgotten the martyr Edith Stein and her foresight. She was an

> *"The world needs what women are!"* –Edith Stein

extraordinarily prolific and productive author; her complete works number twenty-eight volumes, with most published posthumously. Her philosophical works, essays on women's education, and writings on mysticism and spirituality were groundbreaking. Her St. Thomas Aquinas and John Henry Newman translations helped spread their Catholic teachings.

In 1995, an award-winning movie entitled Edith Stein: *The Seventh Chamber* was produced to share the incredible story of this philosopher and Catholic convert. The film shows how her Jewish upbringing, united with her search for the truth, brought her to the Catholic faith. In the movie, Edith was portrayed by Romanian Jewish actress Maia Morgenstern, who would later portray the Blessed Virgin Mary in *The Passion of the Christ*, released in 2004, breaking many box office records.

In 1998, Pope St. John Paul II (*Power Priest* chapter 3) canonized her. St. Teresa Benedicta of the Cross is now one of the six patron saints of Europe. The other five are as follows:

1. St. Benedict of Nursia
2. St Bridget of Sweden
3. St. Catherine of Sienna
4. St. Cyril
5. St. Methodius

The latter two saints were brothers who devised the Cyrillic alphabet for the Slavic people and translated the Bible into their native language to evangelize them. Notably and of similar prowess, three of the six patrons are women, demonstrating the truth in Edith's quote that women are what the world needs.

Two decades after Allied troops freed the prisoners of these death camps, Carmelite nuns deliberately chose the former Dachau concentration camp for a convent. This place of horror would become a place of offering and prayer and a symbol of hope.

CHAPTER CHALLENGE

FAITH CHALLENGE

- Edith Stein underwent several intellectual and spiritual transformations and conversions throughout her life. Her pursuit of knowledge brought her closer to Christ. Learn the roots of the Catholic faith by understanding the Jewish influence in the Old Testament. Start by learning the Ten Commandments* given by God to Moses:

  1. I am the Lord your God: You shall not have strange Gods before me.
  2. You shall not take the name of the Lord your God in vain.
  3. Remember to keep holy the Lord's Day.
  4. Honor your father and mother.
  5. You shall not kill.
  6. You shall not commit adultery.
  7. You shall not steal.
  8. You shall not bear false witness against your neighbors.
  9. You shall not covet your neighbor's wife.
  10. You shall not covet your neighbor's goods.

  *Source: Catechism of the Catholic Church based on Exodus 20:2-17 and Deuteronomy 5:6-21

WORKS CHALLENGE

- Study hard, discover, and develop the gifts God is giving you to be more effective in helping others.

CHAPTER 3

SISTER MARY ANTONA EBO
POWER SOCIAL ACTIVIST

> *"Do what the Spirit moves you."*
> – Sr. Mary Antona Ebo

On Good Friday, April 12, 1963, Dr. Martin Luther King Jr. (MLK) led a march from the 16th Street Baptist Church toward City Hall in Birmingham, Alabama. He was almost immediately arrested, charged with violating a court order, and taken to jail.

The short march and subsequent arrest were part of a series of events in Alabama that helped bring justice for all in what MLK called the most racially segregated city in America. Despite the U.S. Supreme Court ruling nearly a decade earlier that such segregation was unconstitutional, Alabama schools had just desegregated, and fewer than 2% of African Americans were registered to vote due to state laws targeting minorities.

Two years later, Catholic Sister Mary Antona Ebo of St. Louis, who had just recently voted in her hometown, would become a reluctant face and voice for the movement towards fairer voting rights. Raised Baptist, Sister Ebo shared a foundational faith with MLK and his dream for equal rights for all despite the slow progress in some areas of the United States.

The movement for equality had taken many steps and, unfortunately, many decades, but some of the more recent events that led up to the march Sister Ebo joined in 1965 included the following:

- 1954 U.S. Supreme Court declared segregation unconstitutional in Brown v. Board of Education
- 1962, Alabama elected Governor George Wallace, who declared, "Segregation now! Segregation tomorrow! Segregation forever!"
- 1963 The University of Alabama and Alabama high schools desegregate, and President John F. Kennedy sends National Guard troops to ensure compliance by Governor Wallace
- 1963, MLK led marches in Birmingham, Alabama, where four children were killed at a church.
- 1964 The U.S. passed the Civil Rights Act.
- 1964 (July) Alabama banned mass church meetings and public protests about voting rights.
- 1965 (March 7) A peaceful march in Selma, Alabama, by 600 protesting the voting restrictions, ended with 50 in the hospital when state troopers used tear gas and clubs to stop the march. It would become known as "Bloody Sunday" and spur national support after being televised nationally.
- 1965 (March 10), Sister Ebo and thousands of others arrive in Selma, Alabama, to re-step the route planned on Bloody Sunday.

Before sharing more about the march, where one of the police officers on site referred to Sister Ebo as "the beautiful black nun" to reporters, let's explore her personal journey to her vocation.

Sister Ebo was born Elizabeth Louise on April 10, 1924, in Bloomington, Illinois. Her family called her Betty Lou; her mother taught her about God and baptized her in the Baptist Church. Her mom died when she was four years old, and her father lost his job as a library janitor shortly after that. Unable to keep their home, her father put her and her two siblings in a children's home and placed them in programs to train for labor jobs.

In the home, a boy nicknamed "Bishop" was the first to expose Elizabeth to Catholicism. He wasn't allowed to practice his faith in the home openly, but that didn't stop him. One day, he and Elizabeth were sent on an errand to pick up some day-old bread. On the way, he slipped into a Catholic church, knelt at the Communion rail, and prayed. Sister Ebo recalls:

"Bishop was longing for his church. I cased the joint, and it was beautiful. The sun shone through the stained-glass windows that day, and I knew all those stories. I was interested in everything in that church... Bishop explained while he knelt at the Communion rail about this little house (tabernacle) where Jesus was kept, and that the bread became Jesus during the words in Scripture–that was the difference... Communion in the Catholic Church becomes the body and blood of Jesus Christ, and nobody else was telling me that."

On that day, at the tender age of 9, Elizabeth knew she would be Catholic one day.

As a child, she battled tuberculosis in her thumb and was in and out of the hospital for treatment. While in the hospital, Elizabeth asked nurse Mary Southwick if a visiting priest could come by her room. The priest and nurse would become pivotal figures in her life, teaching her about Catholicism and later helping her get into Holy Trinity Catholic High School in Bloomington.

Elizabeth and other children at the home.

Having lost a friend around the same time she lost her mother, Elizabeth wanted to ensure she did everything she could to get to heaven. So, she became a Catholic to partake in the Eucharist.

POWER SISTERS | 37

> *"Truly, truly, I say to you. Unless you eat of the flesh of the son of man, you have no life within you."*
> –John 6:53

The children's home where Elizabeth had been staying did not welcome her back once she decided to join the Catholic Church. As a result, she was sent to live with a couple of older African-American women, where she stayed until she finished high school. She was the first African-American to graduate from her high school.

After graduating high school, Elizabeth wanted to attend a nursing school but was rejected because of her race. She remembers, "They told me they had never admitted a colored girl before." School officials didn't talk to her about her previous studies or academic capabilities but focused on her skin color. Sister Ebo remembers experiences like this as "bruises" she carried throughout life. Sister Ebo showed that God's law is supreme through civil disobedience of immoral law.

She entered the United States Cadet Nurse Corps at St. Mary's Infirmary in 1942. It was a three-year program designed to train replacements for volunteer nurses serving in the war. Although Elizabeth never entered the war, her brother served with the Army in the South Pacific during World War II.

After her training, Elizabeth continued to break down barriers and deepen her faith journey as she entered the Sisters of St. Mary in St. Louis. She became Sister Mary Antona (picture on the left), one of the first three African-American women to enter the order.

In 1962, she earned her degree in medical records administration from St. Louis University. After serving as an assistant administrator of St. Mary Infirmary, she became the Director of Medical Records in 1965. The same year she became the first black supervisor ever to oversee any department at St. Mary's, she would march in Selma, Alabama, to help others have similar opportunities.

When Sister Ebo's superior first asked her if she would like to go to Selma after Bloody Sunday, she answered, "No, I would not like to go to Selma. I know I do a lot of fussing, but I don't feel bad enough to want to go down there and be a martyr for somebody's rights."

She realized it was bigger than voting rights as she said those words. It was the right to be self-determining and have the opportunities that she had. All the same, Sister Ebo was terrified. Her faith soon trumped her fear. She would later share, "It is one thing to have a right on a piece of paper, but if you cannot express that right in the way you live, the way you vote, the way you are self-determining, something has to give."

For her, the question of getting involved in social justice is answered in Matthew 25:31-46 when Jesus says, "Whatever you did for one of these least brothers of mine, you did for me." She felt that she had to take a position, and that position had to be based on faith. As a Catholic, she felt it was her responsibility to meet her brothers and sisters in Christ and "realize we all come from the same God." She felt she was " responsible for speaking up and becoming part of the response." Her response was supported by the Second Vatican Council, which encouraged sisters to get out of their ivory towers, out of their habits, and into the communities they were serving.

She joined 50 delegates from St. Louis as the largest contingent to respond to Dr. King's call for religious leaders to come to Selma and enter the second attempt to march to Montgomery. Sister Ebo was one of only six nuns and the only African-American woman in the group. Leaders from various denominations joined the sisters and priests and arrived in Selma on March 10th. When Sister Ebo stepped off the plane in Selma, a priest there thought,

> "Oh my God. This is going to make a difference."

People were surprised to see the six sisters. There were forty-eight brothers and quite a few priests, but the nuns, particularly one, stole the show.

They met the rest of the marchers at Brown Chapel AME, where crowds parted as minister Andrew Young introduced Sister Ebo. He exclaimed, "Ladies and gentlemen, one of the great moral forces of the world has just stepped into the door!" Everybody turned around and gave a standing ovation. Sr. Ebo realized she was sitting in the Pastor's chair.

She was scared, but her determination and faith were stronger. The Lord will make a way somehow, and she felt she had to keep going. Earlier, she had left her mantle on the plane, but she went back, worried that she might get cold in jail without it if she were arrested.

The St. Louis group was asked to lead the march that day, with the sisters front and center. They led the way as the group set out on the second attempt to cross over Edmund Pettus Bridge on the way to Montgomery. The sisters had men surrounding them for their protection. The men feared the crowd would push the sisters forward, so they had their backs. But the group didn't get far.

The bridge was not opened to them. In fact, the mayor stopped them before they reached the line of state troopers just ahead. He reminded them of the law against marching in protest and said he expected it to be followed. Then, someone thought the religious leaders should "bear witness" to why they were marching. Then, Sister Ebo became an icon when a broadcaster recorded an exchange between her and local government agents.

She told them:
"We are here from St. Louis to demonstrate and to witness our love to our fellow citizens in Selma. We are here, secondly, to protest the violation of rights... I feel it a privilege to be here today. I am Sister Mary Antona, and... yesterday, I voted. And I'd like to come here today and say that every citizen should be given the right to vote. That's why I'm here today."

The entire group then knelt to say the Our Father and made their way back to the church. Their march was short, but their impact was immense.

Finally, a federal court order was issued to allow the march, and President L.B. Johnson pledged his support. U.S. Army troops protected the marchers on their four-day journey to Montgomery. The image of Sister Ebo marching in Selma that day would become an icon. She remembers:

"It turned out that the habit was what got everyone's attention very quickly because nuns had not been seen doing anything like that before. It didn't ring a bell with me that we were getting involved in something hysterical and historical."

The day after the march, she was back on duty, attending Mass at 6 a.m. and serving at the hospital. Various media outlets, including the Vatican newspaper, contacted her, and she took the new attention as a humble servant of God.

Within five months of the march, the U.S. passed the Voting Rights Act, which aimed to overcome the legal barriers at the state and local levels that had prevented African Americans from exercising their right to vote under the Fifteenth Amendment (1870) to the Constitution of the United States.

Sister Ebo said, *"The one thing I didn't want to do was to become a sweet little old nun that was passing out holy cards and telling people 'I'll pray for you' and not really having mastered or developed an expertise in being a caregiver from a good theological base."*

Inspired by the success of the march, Sister Ebo continued to promote justice and equal rights elsewhere. When she returned home to St. Louis, she helped found the National Black Sisters' Conference.

"If you really want peace, work for justice."
– Pope Paul VI

Turning her efforts specifically to promoting healthcare, she earned her master's degree in hospital executive development from St. Louis University in 1970, and in 1976, she was appointed as the executive director of the St. Clare Hospital in Baraboo, Wisconsin. She became the first African-American religious woman to head any Catholic Hospital nationwide.

After some health problems of her own, she decided she wanted to get out of administration and into a more theological approach to healthcare. So, she earned her second master's degree, this time in Theology of Health Care in 1978 from Aquinas Institute of Theology and began serving as a hospital chaplain.

Her devotion to caring for others began to bring her attention. In 1989, the National Black Sisters' Conference presented her with the Harriet Tubman Award and described her as "a Moses to the people."

In 2000, at the 35th anniversary of what came to be known as the "Right to Vote" Bridge Crossing, she was honored with the Living Legend Award by the Voting Rights Institute in Selma.

In 2002, she received the Distinguished Humanitarian Award from the Dr. Martin Luther King, Jr. State Celebration Commission of Missouri. She was honored as the Lifetime Achiever in Health Care by the St. Louis American Foundation in 2012.

Additionally, she has been the recipient of six honorary doctorate degrees from the following universities:

- Loyola University-Chicago (1995)
- College of New Rochelle of New York (2008)
- Aquinas Institute (2009)
- St. Louis University (2010)
- University of Missouri St Louis (2010)
- University of Notre Dame (2013)

On top of her chaplain duties and attending these various award ceremonies and graduations, she continued to speak out for the voting rights of African Americans and all Americans.

Sister Mary Antona Ebo was a legendary civil rights trailblazer. After one of her talks, one person in the audience told her that her talk had changed his life.

She got a standing ovation when she accepted an honorary degree from her alma mater, St. Louis University, at the graduation ceremony in 2010. The applause continued for so long Sister Ebo began to get uncomfortable with the attention.

She then looked upward, pointed to the sky, and shared the words that guided her for decades, *"Give your glory to God. Give your prayers to me."*

Sister Mary Antona Ebo died on November 11, 2017 (Veteran's Day), at 93. Although she was not a veteran, she did fight for freedom, justice, and equality, and in recognition of her stature, the Archbishop of St. Louis presided at her funeral Mass.

> *"Her courage and work to end the injustice of racism provided the inspiration and guidance."*
> – The Archdiocesan Peace and Justice Commission

CHAPTER CHALLENGE

FAITH CHALLENGE

- Learn and explore further the Catholic church's seven principles of social teaching:

  I. Respect the Human Person

  II. Promote the Family

  III. Protect Property Rights

  IV. Work for the Common Good

  V. Observe the Principle of Subsidiarity*

  VI. Respect Work and the Worker

  VII. Pursue Peace and Care for the Poor

  * Subsidiarity is the principle of allowing the individual members of a large organization to make decisions on issues that affect them rather than leaving those decisions to be made by the whole group. It is primarily applied to balancing government versus individual citizen rights and duties.

- Learn about current issues and the Church's position on them from websites like Catholic.com

  Consider reading other sources:
  - Compendium of the Social Doctrine of the Church (available online from www.vatican.va)
  - Introduction to Catholic Social Teaching by Fr. Rodger Charles, S.J. (Ignatius)

WORKS CHALLENGE

- Find a way to apply the Catholic Church's social teaching principles in your family or community. Make the actions and words of Jesus real again today by uplifting the lives of all people as outlined in the Gospels.

CHAPTER 4

MOTHER ANGELICA
POWER TELEVISION BROADCASTER

> *"Faith is one foot on the ground, one foot in the air, and a queasy feeling in the stomach."* – Mother Angelica

As the child of an abusive father who abandoned her mother and her, Rita Rizzo's humble beginning showed little indication that the woman who would become Mother Angelica would establish a media network to take her Father in Heaven's message of love to the world.

Born in the southeastern part of Canton, Ohio, known for its slums and red-light district run by mobsters, young Rita was only five years old when her dad left the family. Life became extremely hard for Rita and her mom, and they never had enough money or food. When Rita turned six, the United States entered modern history's most prolonged and deepest economic downturn. It lasted more than a decade, from 1929 to 1941, leaving many Americans unemployed and in poverty.

Under the weight of raising a child as a divorced single mother during the Great Depression, Rita's mom became severely depressed, limiting her ability to work or even function. So, Rita helped provide for the family. Rita could barely

> *"We were poor, hungry, and barely surviving on odd jobs. We pinched pennies just to keep food on the table."*
> – Mother Angelica

POWER SISTERS | 47

see over the dashboard as an eleven-year-old, but she drove her mother's car to deliver dry cleaning to earn money.

Fortunately, a local priest, Father Joseph Riccardi, occasionally helped the family. But when Fr. Joe challenged the mafia, he was shot in the vestibule of his parish by a twenty-seven-year-old woman accompanied by her five-year-old daughter. Fr. Joe died later that same day. The judge found the shooter not guilty at the trial since the mafia also controlled the courts. His early death brought more grief to the family, which was already struggling.

After this sad event, a feeling of being ostracized as a divorced Catholic, and some cruel words from a missionary priest who misinterpreted the church's teaching on divorce during a confession, Rita and her mother left the Catholic Church for over a decade. The Church, which had been a source of strength for the struggling family, had become too much of a source of pain. Rita and her mother eventually moved in with her maternal grandparents during her teenage years. Still, when her grandfather suffered a stroke, leaving him paralyzed on one side of his body, Rita once again helped with chores.

While attending McKinley High School in Canton, Rita struggled academically. Her mind was preoccupied with caring for her family and whether her mother had committed suicide that day. Rita did not socialize much or date out of fear of neglecting her mother, but she joined the school's band as one of the first two female drum majorettes.

Little did anyone realize when she graduated in 1941 that this school named for Anna McKinley, the sister of the 25th United States President William McKinley and a teacher for thirty years, would produce one of the most outstanding teachers of the

Catholic faith. The struggling student would follow the example of the school's mascot and bulldog her way to start a global Catholic television network forty years later.

During her senior year of high school, Rita started suffering from a painful stomach problem that made it difficult for her to eat or even sleep. Rita worked through the pain since, in December of 1941, the Japanese attack on Pearl Harbor dragged the United States into the worldwide conflict of WWII, and everyone needed to support the effort.

In a steel-producing town like Canton, the war brought jobs, and Rita joined the ranks of women on the wartime payroll. She became the secretary of the vice president of advertising for a company producing gun barrels. She wrote, edited, and organized advertising campaigns and even learned to operate some of the heavy machinery forging the steel.

After suffering from the stomach affliction for over two years and losing twenty pounds, Rita visited a Catholic mystic after the advice of a friend. The mystic woman, who as a stigmatic endured some of the same bodily pains as Christ did during his passion, encouraged Rita to pray a nine-day novena to Saint Therese of Lisieux, the Little Flower. On the last day of the novena, Rita woke up during the night feeling like someone was pulling her stomach out of her. The stomach pain was gone when she awakened the following day, and she had a renewed faith in God.

Rita celebrated by asking her grandmother to cook her a pork chop. When questioned how she could finally eat something she had not been able to for years, Rita lifted her pajama top, showing the blue coloration on her midsection was gone. Her younger cousin hit her stomach to prove she was completely healed.

> *"We may encounter defeat, but we must not be defeated."*
> –Maya Angelou

After this miraculous healing, Rita came to believe that God did love her. When she returned to the Church, she felt a pull to serve God. She shared, "I knew that God knew me and loved me. All I wanted to do after my healing was give myself to Jesus."

Rita adopted a series of devotional practices which prepared her for her future religious vocation.

- Had only tea and crackers every Saturday.
- Read spiritual literature daily.
- Recited the Way of the Cross daily.
- Met with a spiritual director regularly.
- Erected an altar with two large statues of the Sacred Heart and the Blessed Mother in her bedroom.

After completing the Way of the Cross at a side altar in her parish church, Rita knelt facing the statue of Our Lady of Sorrows and felt a deep awareness that she had a vocation. She knew then that she had to go wherever the Lord would send her. She met with a priest who affirmed her call and agreed to not share with her mother, who was still struggling emotionally, particularly after learning about the re-marriage of her ex-husband to a classmate of Rita's half his age.

Since Rita's grades in high school were so poor, none of the teaching orders would accept her. So, her options were limited. To avoid telling her mother, she secretly traveled to Buffalo, New York, to visit the Josephite nuns who worked with the deaf. Although the Josephite order accepted her, the priest guiding her suggested that God wanted her to join a cloistered Franciscan monastery in Cleveland. Once again, to avoid telling her mother, her boss took her to and from the bus station for her day visit to the St. Paul Shrine in Cleveland.

> *"When you have God, you don't have to know everything about it; you just do it."* –Mother Angelica

The next day, after describing the wonders of the monastery to her close friend, Rita made plans to join the order. She also started a letter to her mother, which she would mail after she entered the cloistered order. She wrote how much she loved and appreciated her mother while acknowledging the shock she would feel reading the letter. Rita assured her that this was God's call and emphasized, "A cloister, my mother is a heaven on earth."

Her mother took the news with tears and anger, even as she read she could visit her every two months. Not even a gentle reminder from her daughter that "we belong first to God and then our parents; we are his children." could ease the initial pain in her mother's heart. A year later, her mother came to peace with her vocation after visiting Rita on her twenty-second birthday. She wrote in her diary, "I offer Thee my beloved daughter."

Rita now had her mother's blessing, and years later, her superior would give her mother the honor of choosing her religious name. Since Rita had been an "angelic and obedient daughter" in her eyes, she chose Angelica even though subduing the brash side of her personality sometimes proved challenging.

That brash side of Sister Angelica would be put to practical use by her abbess, Mother Clare, who put her in charge of renovating a house donated to the order in her hometown of Canton, Ohio. These construction projects would help the new head of the house,

POWER SISTERS | 51

Mother Angelica, develop her leadership skills and bring her back in contact with her dad.

As a cloistered nun, Sister Angelica had limited access to outsiders. As mentioned, family members could only visit every other month, but after one day on the renovation worksite, her father stopped by the convent. Seeing her dirty hands, her dad insisted he bring her special soap. When he brought back the cleaning supplies, he added an apology for being an absent father. He would die six months later, but his apology brought her peace and closure to her childhood woes.

Her challenging childhood would ironically serve as a training ground for her future roles. The skills she developed going to her derelict dad for money since he was frequently late on child support payments served as a springboard to her future fundraising efforts. First, though, Sister Angelica had to endure another health issue before hearing her call to leave Ohio.

While operating some cleaning equipment at the monastery, Mother Angelica slipped and hurt her back. She endured the pain for the next few years by offering it to God, but eventually, doctors suggested a remedy. Although risky due to the proximity to the spine, surgery could provide relief. The determined nun made a deal with God. If the surgery was successful, she would open a new convent in the South where Protestant faiths dominated.

"No matter what our problems are, Jesus can stop them in a second." –Mother Angelica

The surgery was a success, and Mother Angelica now had to make good on her promise. After some visits to Florida and other southern states, she received an invitation from the Bishop of Mobile, Alabama. With the assistance of Birmingham's former mayor, Mother Angelica found ten acres of gently sloping mountain-side land in Irondale, an ideal setting for a monastery. When she discovered the house next door was in foreclosure, she quickly placed a contract on it and the twenty more acres surrounding it.

Although the local zoning board delayed approval of the building permits, the delay gave the Sisters more time to raise money. One fundraising idea landed them in the news and even in an issue of *Sports Illustrated*, a magazine better known for women in swimsuits than habits. Since fishing was extremely popular in the area, the nuns crafted artificial lures. As cloistered nuns, they tested them in a convent bathtub and marketed them under the name of St. Peter's Fishing Lures, an appropriate name since the first Pope was a fisherman before Jesus's call for him to be a fisher of men and rock upon He would build his Church.

By the summer of 1961, twenty years after she had barely graduated from high school, Mother Angelica had the permits and deeds for the land. The purchase cost was thirteen thousand dollars, the precise amount the fishing lure business earned! God rewarded her prayers and patience; fishing lures would not be her last unique fundraising idea.

Over the years, Mother Angelica's monastery sold various divinely inspired items to raise needed funds before moving into satellite television.

- Peanuts, borrowing the idea from a neighbor.
- Books, printing and binding the books themselves.
- Audio and videotapes of Mother Angelica's talks

In Irondale, Alabama, a town just east of Birmingham where racial tensions erupted in violence in the 1950s, construction began on a new home for the Poor Clares of Perpetual Adoration called Our Lady of the Angels Monastery. They hoped to bring peace and the Catholic faith to the region. Although the local bishop shoveled the ceremonial first hole, everyone knew who was in charge once construction began. As one monastery contractor said, "You better see Mother. She's the boss on this job."

When the boss was not on the construction site, she was busy raising funds and getting donations. Her love for people of all faiths meant an ecumenical solution. A Baptist neighbor donated dirt, and a Jewish-owned company supplied all the tile for the building.

On the job site, the many Black protestants and Italian Catholic construction workers admired the hardworking nun. Mother Angelica's hometown had similar ethnic diversity, so she was comfortable interacting with the workers but not afraid to share her displeasure with shoddy work. When the bricklayers were careless with joints, she made them tear down a wall and rebuild it.

In 1962, the same year Vatican II started, Mother Angelica traded her construction hat for her traditional habit. She recorded the first of many talks she would give, entertaining audiences while teaching them about the Catholic faith. The topic was "God's Love for You," and although she spoke from the heart with little preparation, it sold fifteen hundred copies in six months.

> *"I think the best preparation is to have no preparation. Jesus will tell me what to say when the time comes."*
> – Mother Angelica

In September of 1963, as she recorded her second talk entitled "The Presence of God," the need for her presence in Alabama was reinforced by a dynamite attack by the Ku Klux Klan on a Baptist Church in nearby Birmingham. The blast tragically killed four Black girls and injured other parishioners. The event marked a turning point in the United States during the civil rights movement and contributed to support for the passage of the Civil Rights Act of 1964 by Congress, prohibiting racism in public places and in hiring practices.

One thing she knew people needed was prayer, but she believed many did not know how to pray. Although she was already busy leading the sisters, overseeing construction, and recording talks, she felt God calling her to do more. Mother Angelica's first booklet, *Journey into Prayer*, explained prayer as a "union of love: God's love and your love." She asked readers to reflect on this love in seven steps shared at the end of this chapter.

Although she prayed to God that she did not know how to author a book, she and her eleven fellow sisters would go on to publish over fifty booklets and books. After her regular printing company refused to print one of her early books on the Eucharist, the twelve nuns, like the first "stinky apostles" (her words), purchased expensive equipment and moved printing in-house, rolling 25,000 books off the press each day.

POWER SISTERS | 55

One of those sisters included her very own mother, who, after moving to Alabama to be close to her daughter, joined the order as Sister Mary David. The woman who a young Rita called mother was now calling her mother.

Although having her mother in her order presented Mother Angelica with some unique challenges, especially as her mother's health declined, her busy travel schedule continued. A seven-day trip to Chicago in 1978 would decisively change her life forever.

While touring a Baptist-run television station atop a Chicago skyscraper, Mother Angelica quickly realized the power of television communication to reach a broader audience. She whispered in prayer, "Lord, I gotta have one of these." As a cloistered nun, she did not know anything about television, but that nor the million-dollar price tag of the studio deterred her since she had intuition and God on her side.

> *"Unless you are willing to do the ridiculous, God will not do the miraculous."* – Mother Angelica

After the local CBS studio that was airing some of her talks also aired a fraudulent miniseries entitled *The Word*, casting doubt on the divinity of Jesus Christ, Mother Angelica was inspired to start her own network. The Eternal Word Television Network (EWTN) would advance the "truth as defined by the Magisterium of the Roman Catholic Church."

With no budget and only two hundred dollars in the bank, the determined nun made plans to build a studio and ordered a large satellite dish. She teamed up with two attorneys to secure broadcasting licenses from the Federal Communication Commission (FCC) and draft bylaws for the new non-profit EWTN. A protestant TV evangelist dispatched a team to build her first studio, a powder blue living room in the convent's garage.

Unfortunately, Mother Angelica had not yet secured a benefactor to donate the $600,000 needed as a down payment for the thirty-three-foot satellite dish. When deliverymen arrived, they refused to unload the dish until they collected the money. Mother stalled for time by retreating to the chapel, thinking she had blown it.

Shortly after she emerged, one of the sisters called her to the phone. A wealthy donor was calling from his yacht in the Bahamas and said that because one of her books helped him deal with his troubled children, he was sending her a check for six hundred thousand dollars. He agreed to wire it, and the satellite was unloaded before lunch!

The next forty years would bring tremendous growth and challenges for Mother Angelic and her EWTN team. Still, for years, the most popular show on the network was *Mother Angelica Live,* where her practical advice and feisty humor endeared her to viewers. After she suffered a stroke in 2001, Mother withdrew from public ministry and led a life of prayer until her death on Easter Sunday in 2016.

The network she started in a garage now reaches over 350 million homes in 145 countries and territories. It is the largest religious media network in the world and broadcasts in multiple languages 24 hours a day every day. EWTN platforms include radio, one of the largest Catholic websites, electronic and print news services, and a book publishing division.

POWER SISTERS | 57

Relying solely on God's providence, Mother Angelica built the Catholic media empire without concern for budgets or significant fund-raising campaigns. Despite some sparring with U.S. bishops, who at one point had started a competing television network, she had the support of the Vatican. Having launched EWTN shortly after Saint John Paul II was elected to the papacy in 1978, the two had a good relationship. In a private meeting, he reportedly told a Cardinal, "EWTN is the key to restoring the Roman Catholic Church in America."

The child of a broken home who struggled academically accomplished what many considered impossible because she had great faith in God. One Catholic bishop described her as her generation's Venerable Archbishop Fulton Sheen, an Emmy-winning theologian.

Seeing EWTN as a beacon for theological clarity and a safe port for the average Catholic, she stayed true to the teachings of Jesus in scripture and the traditions of the Catholic faith. When questioned about the seemingly limited role of women, she quipped, "Women have more power in the Church than anybody. They built and run the schools." She recognized that true power did not come from a title but from what the Holy Spirit can accomplish through her.

CHAPTER CHALLENGE

FAITH CHALLENGE

- Connect weekly with Catholic media. Find a show or podcast that helps you learn the faith, but first reflect on the following from Mother Angelica's first booklet in prayer to understand God's love for you:
    - God's love for me is as if no one else existed.
    - His love for me is beyond description.
    - He knew me and loved me before He created anything.
    - I am important to God; therefore, He sent His Son to live and die for me.
    - He made me His dwelling place on earth at Baptism.
    - He nourishes my soul with His own Body and Blood in the Eucharist.
    - God dwells in me and longingly waits for my expressions of love.

> *"Those who tell you the truth love you. Those who tell you what you want to hear love themselves."*
> – Mother Angelica

WORKS CHALLENGE

- Find a way to help others in a world that so desperately needs it. As three-time U.S. Olympian Dominique Dawes suggested in this article linked below, ask Mother Angelica how we can emulate what she did, even in a smaller way.

For more on this remarkable woman, check out Raymond Arroyo's biography of her.

CHAPTER 5

SISTER DEDE BYRNE POSC
POWER VETERAN AND SURGEON

> *"I am a religious sister and a surgeon. I serve Christ in the poor and was able to care for our incredible soldiers."*
> – Sister Dede Byrne

Sister Deirdre "Dede" Mary Byrne may have entered the religious life later in life, but her parents planted the seeds of the Catholic faith early in her life. Her mother stayed home, raised eight children, and said that Dede was destined for the religious life even in the womb.

Her 6'3" father played football at the University of Notre Dame and became a thoracic surgeon and chief of surgery at Fairfax Hospital in Virginia. Sister Dede

> *"Our parents are the best catechists."*
> – Sr. Dede Byrne

considers both parents heroes for their love of faith and family. Despite their busy schedules, both attended Mass daily, even on family vacations. Those vacations sometimes also included hospital visits where her father cared for those in need.

Her childhood in Virginia was generally carefree. With her seven siblings, she loved the outdoors and played in the creeks near their home. They enjoyed playing baseball, and she especially enjoyed climbing trees. Climbing trees would foreshadow her rise

POWER SISTERS | 63

through the ranks in the military and her successful career as a physician and later surgeon, but as a young child, she had to overcome one major obstacle first.

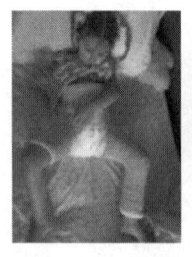

Due to a congenital dislocated hip, Dede had to wear a body cast from her hip to her lower leg for a year. Her siblings would drag her around and use her cast and leg as a step stool to reach things on high shelves. So, despite the inconvenience, she learned early on in life that being stepped on was not always a terrible thing since it could lift others up, a foreshadowing of her religious vows.

Her parents were very generous to the Catholic Church and their overseas missions. Because of their donations, the family always had magazines from the Maryknoll missions around the house. Young Dede would sit around and look through these magazines, fascinated by the generous work of Catholic missionaries like Mother Teresa of Calcutta, now St. Teresa. She felt missionary work was the direction God was calling her.

Although that inner desire to enter religious life never disappeared, Dede dated to make sure. She graduated from Langley High School in Fairfax and Virginia Tech before pursuing one of her career goals, following in her father's footsteps, and entering medical school at Georgetown University. Her older brother was also already in his third year of medical school there. Dede wanted to take some of the financial burden off her parents, who, in addition to the two children in medical school, were already supporting four other children in college. The United States Army, she found out, just happened to have a great scholarship program for medical school students.

Having minimal exposure to the military as a child, Dede admits she had no clue what she was getting herself into, but she trusted the idea came from God. She initially acknowledged that it was not very altruistic of her since she joined to pay for school, but she fell in love with the Army after joining. She fell in love with her fellow soldiers and became even more patriotic.

> *"If you just totally open yourself up to God's will, you've just got to put your seat belt on, and you're going to be up for a wild ride."*
> – Sister Dede Byrne

One of those siblings who benefited from the financial burden she took off her parents was the youngest, William, who was attending the College of Holy Cross at the time. After becoming a popular columnist and YouTube personality, Fr. Bill was appointed the 10th Bishop of Springfield, Massachusetts, in 2020.

After finishing medical school, Dede paid back her Army obligation as a Captain and soon experienced her first miracle with a patient in a coma for a month. While stationed in South Korea, Captain Byrne, M.D. accompanied a woman who had been in a coma for months on a Medevac from South Korea to the United States. A Medevac is short for a medical *evacuation* of military or other *casualties* to the hospital in a helicopter or airplane.

During the long plane trip, Captain Byrne prayed over her patient while she monitored her vitals. As she and the patient's daughter looked on, the patient woke up midway through the three-day journey. This incident reminded her that God was really in charge, and He was uniquely calling her. A nun in South Korea reinforced that calling by telling her, "You are Jesus's doctor."

She was blessed to care for patients and soldiers all over the world, including in Korea, Iraq, Afghanistan, Egypt's Sinia peninsula, Sudan, and her own backyard in Washington, D.C., where she spent most of her military career.

> *"Amen, I say to you, whatever you did for one of these least brothers of mine, you did for me"*
> – Matthew 25:40

While in North Africa, Dr. Byrne was a family doctor and became the liaison for the monks at St. Catherine's Monastery at the foot of Mount Sinia, where Moses received the tablets with the Ten Commandments. The monks had been in the region since the fourth century and appreciated having a Catholic doctor care for them.

In Sudan, she cared for the local civilians whose villages were bombed by the Sudanese every Sunday. She often cared for these innocent civilians who were missing limbs after the bombings. The atrocities devastated her and reminded her of our constant battle against evil. God may have been preparing her for other ways she would witness man's inhumanity to man.

> *"Our battle is not between political parties, but between Good and evil."*
> – Sister Dede Byrne

After nine years on active duty, Dr. Byrne joined the Army reserves for the remainder of her military career. That first year off active duty, she spent performing missionary medicine in India, where she met and worked with her high school hero, St. Teresa of Calcutta.

After twenty years as an emergency and family practice physician, Dr. Byrne returned to Georgetown University for a second residency since she could not decide whether to stay in family medicine or pursue her passion for surgery. The return gave her two unique opportunities.

In 1997, Dr. Byrne served as Mother Teresa's personal doctor when she made her final visit to the United States just six weeks before her death. During that visit, the now St. Teresa of Calcutta received the Congressional Gold Medal in D.C. and met with Princess Diana in New York City. The two would pass away within days of each other. The Congressional Gold Medal is the highest civilian award in the United States, alongside the Presidential Medal of Freedom. It seeks to impart the highest expression of national appreciation for distinguished achievements and contributions by individuals or institutions.

That same year, Dr. Byrne served on the medical team that provided care for Cardinal James Hickey. He was the Archbishop of Washington D.C. at the time and served for twenty years from 1980 to 2000. As the chief resident on the cardiac surgery team, Dr. Byrne used the time while he recovered at Georgetown to get to know Cardinal Hickey, and he became her spiritual director.

These chance encounters to serve would continue after she finished her second residency and became a surgeon. God placed her where she was needed. On Sep 11, 2001, the now Colonel Byrne M.D. was in New York City when al-Qaeda, a terrorist organization, hijacked two commercial airplanes and flew them into the twin towers of the World Trade Center. After the towers fell, she assisted victims and firefighters with water and limited medical support.

Although she continued to discern the religious life, Army and medical commitments put her vocation off. Dr. Byrne was clear that she wanted to serve the poor with the best medical training she could get first. Still, she was torn between joining Mother Teresa and her Missionaries of Charity or The Little Workers of the Sacred Hearts of Jesus and Mary close to her home in Washington, D.C.

She just wanted to ensure she chose the right community, being a traditionally-minded, old-fashioned girl. During an hour of adoration before the Blessed Sacrament one day, she asked, "Well, Lord, do you want me to forget about this religious thing or give up being a doctor?" She initially decided on the latter because she knew being a surgeon did not fit with either religious community.

One day, she sat down with an elderly Jesuit friend, Father John Hardon, who told her directly, "You will not join the Missionaries of Charity! God gave you this gift to do medicine. You must use it."

The Little Workers of the Sacred Hearts of Jesus and Mary were founded by Monsignor Francesco Maria Greco (now Blessed) and Sister Maria Teresa DeVincenti in southern Italy in 1892 to educate poor children in the area. The congregation added other apostolates: medical work, the staffing of orphanages, social work, and the care of the aged and infirm in hospitals and nursing homes. In addition to coming to the United States in 1948, they opened convents across Italy and established missionary houses, schools, and novitiates in Argentina, Albania, and India.

The habit-wearing members of this religious community focused on an intense prayer life, ran a physical therapy and eye clinic in Washington D.C., and wore hospital garb when necessary. All three elements appealed to Dr. Byrne. When she found out that while about 80% of its members were educators running schools, 20% provided health care to the neediest, she found her fit.

In 2002, Dr. Byrne entered the Little Workers' formation and took her first vows in 2004. Still in the Army reserves, she was

> "It was before the blessed sacrament that I found the love of Jesus and the power of that love."
> – Blessed Monsignor Francesco Maria Greco

deployed to Afghanistan and received special permission from her superior to go and wear the uniform as a soldier sister.

While deployed to Afghanistan, in addition to caring for the medical needs of soldiers deployed to ensure that the country would not again become a haven for international terrorists, she also witnessed local people in the Muslim region convert to Catholicism. When some local Muslims saw her with a small group of fellow Catholics praying, they inquired about her faith. She shared her Catholic traditions and truths, and quite a few were soon baptized.

In 2009, her mother general asked Sister Dede, "Do you think you can retire from the Army?" So, after twenty-nine years of service in the U.S. Army, she retired as a Colonel, the highest rank below a General. When asked whether serving in the military and serving as a Catholic sister was a conflict, she admittedly retorts, "None whatsoever; if you spend any time in the military, you become very patriotic, and as a physician, you are on the healing end of any conflict."

The nun with a gun adds that many people in the military are very devout Catholics. She compliments the priest chaplains who went beyond their official duties and put themselves in harm's way to administer the sacraments.

POWER SISTERS | 69

She also pointed out that the military is a fantastic mission field where many vocations are born, exemplified by three priests in the book, *Power Priests*.

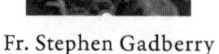

Fr. Stephen Gadberry    Fr. James Flynn    Fr. Richard Sutter

Sister Dede's overseas service continued as a religious missionary to Kenya, Haiti, and Iraq after the military. In Kenya, she served in a clinic and installed water purification treatment centers to help prevent waterborne diseases. Twice a year, she flies to Haiti to provide medical aid and goes to Iraq to help build a hospital in the Kurdish area.

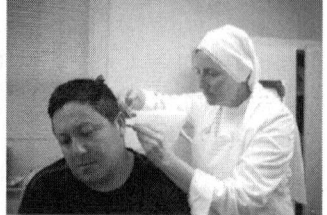

Closer to home, she continues doing general surgeries, mostly on refugee outpatients at the Catholic Charities' medical clinic in Washington D.C. She also manages an elderly home full of retired sisters who she calls "prayer warriors" while supervising interns who she refers to as "baby doctors" at a local hospital. She promotes the ideology that healthcare providers must focus on the well-being of the body and the soul.

> *"Make it your daily mission to be in the state of grace so you can hear God more clearly."*
> –Sister Dede Byrne

In recent years, she has also become a regular speaker at healthcare conferences and even advocated for unborn children on national television. Gaining strength during daily Eucharistic adoration, Sister Dede has advocated for the largest marginalized group in the United States, the child in the mother's womb. Her weapon of choice is now her voice and the rosary.

She regularly encourages audiences to pray for our government leaders and points out that the rosary has fifty Hail Marys over the five decades. Those who pray it can say a Hail Mary for each of the fifty states now that Roe vs. Wade was overturned and pro-life legislation is in the hands of each state. As a physician, she can say unequivocally that life begins at conception.

In 2020 as she was praying about doing more for life. She asked, "Lord, let me be your voice for life." The White House called two hours later, asking her to speak at the Republican National Convention. She shared her experiences at ground zero of the battle for human life in the mother's womb with the national television audience. She calls all to stand for Christ and life.

> "I'm not just pro-life; I'm pro-eternal-life."
> – Sister Dede Byrne

Sister Dede points to the example of St. Joan of Arc, who put on the armor of God when battling evil and encourages all pro-life advocates to follow her example when battling groups like Planned Parenthood who told one of her patients she had to have an abortion

POWER SISTERS | 71

since she would be an unworthy mother. They would not even show the mother the ultrasound of her child.

> *"Put on the armor of God so that you may be able to stand firm against the tactics of the devil. For our struggle is not with flesh and blood but with the principalities, with the powers, with the world rulers of this present darkness."*
> –Ephesians 6:12

When Sister Dede Byrne receives awards and gratitude for her service as a soldier, surgeon, and sister, she gives all glory to God. Since true humility recognizes that one should not bury one's gifts but use those gifts as God intended without being prideful about it.

She plays down the three-part description and awards since humility is part of her order, but she does say, "Lord, if this maybe brings more information about the Little Workers of the Sacred Hearts, that is good." When talking about her work and the work of her fellow sisters, she simply states, "We just do the best we can."

CHAPTER CHALLENGE

FAITH CHALLENGE

- As Sister Dede Byrne recommends spending time in front of the Eucharist when discerning any decision in life. Try finding twenty minutes a week, even if it means simply staying after or going early before Mass to do so.

    Consider praying as she does before giving talks.

    Holy Spirit inspires me. Love of God consume me. To the true pass, lead me. Mary, my mother, look down upon me with Jesus bless me from all evil, from all illusions, from all dangers preserve me. Amen.

- Come up with your own prayer to God that you can pray like Sister Dede Byrne.

WORKS CHALLENGE

- Find a way to help the pro-life movement. Sister Byrne advises first praying and then joining other heroes praying and working to protect all lives. Consider joining a life vigil 40 days for life.

- Maryknoll Missions is a Catholic non-profit that has been the heart and hands of the U.S. Catholic Church's overseas mission work for over one hundred years. Consider supporting their work.

CHAPTER 6

MOTHER DOLORES HART O.S.B.

POWER MOVIE STAR

> "Life has a bigger meaning than you think it does. Every human being has a mission, and you cannot just stop with making movies as a be-all-end-all."
> –Mother Dolores Hart

The woman who gave the legendary musician Elvis Presley his first on screen kiss became a cloistered Benedictine sister, and sixty years later, Mother Dolores Hart still makes it very clear that God is the bigger Elvis.

Born Dolores Hicks in Chicago, Illinois, she was the only child of actor Bert Hicks and Harriett Hicks. Because her parents were both teenagers, her paternal grandmother wanted her mother to have an abortion. Harriett chose life, and a beautiful young girl would start her journey to serve God via Hollywood.

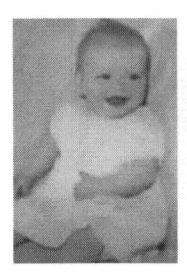

POWER SISTERS | 75

Following acting offers, her father moved his family to Hollywood, California. After visiting her father on his sets, Dolores knew she wanted to become an actress.

> *"It was not a lifelong dream. I did not grow up wanting to be a nun. I wanted to be an actress. If it had ever been suggested I would one day be a nun, it would have been the last thing on my mind."* –Mother Dolores Hart

After her parents divorced, Dolores moved back to Chicago and lived with her grandparents, who sent her to St. Gregory Catholic School. Her grandfather, who operated the projectors at their local movie theater, kindled her enthusiasm for films.

Dolores converted to Catholicism when she was ten, partly because she wanted to join other students for chocolate milk and sweet rolls after they fasted for Mass. She moved to Beverly Hills, California, to live with her mother the following year. She attended the first Catholic high school in the San Fernando Valley, founded by Religious Sisters of the Sacred Heart. At Corvallis, Dolores became involved in acting at the all-girls high school appropriately located in Studio City.

She continued her studies at nearby Marymount College and, at age eighteen, signed a movie contract with Hal Wallis, the producer best known for such hit classics as *Casablanca* and *The Adventures of Robin Hood*. Other stars in his studio at Warner Brothers included acting legends Humphrey Bogart and John Wayne. Dolores earned her first movie role as the love interest of singing sensation Elvis Presley in *Loving You*. Using the stage name Dolores Hart, the nineteen-year-old was grateful to have her prayers answered and get selected from among many young women auditioning for the role.

The naive young actress admitted that she did not know who Elvis was before meeting him and asked him what he did. He was very courteous and, calling her Miss Dolores, said he was a singer. He was always a gentleman, and by the time they did their second film together, *King Creole,* they could not walk down the street together because so many people just wanted to touch him.

Although their kissing scene for *Loving You* was the last scene of the film, the director made it the first thing they did on set. With about one hundred people on the soundstage, Dolores prepared to put her arms around Elvis and kiss him, but seconds into filming, the director yelled, "Cut!" Dolores thought she was kissing wrong, but after the makeup man fixed her up, she found her ears were red from blushing. She was so embarrassed. After fixing Dolores up, they started again, but the director soon yelled, "Cut! Get some makeup for Mister Presley!" When she looked at her famous co-star, she noticed he was blushing red too!

At age twenty-two, Elvis was still a young man exploring his faith. During one break from filming, Elvis handed Dolores a Bible and asked, "Miss Dolores, would you open this book? What do you see? What does it mean to you?" She shared her opinion, and the two spent time between the scenes talking about the Bible. She never expected a fellow actor to have that kind of genuine curiosity, but the future nun not only kissed Elvis, but she evangelized to him.

After starring alongside leading men like Montgomery Clift, Anthony Quinn, and Marlon Brando, Dolores was hailed as the next Grace Kelly. Along with the two movies with Elvis, Dolores Hart was best known for her roles in *Where the Boys Are (1960), Francis of Assisi (1961),* and *Come Fly with Me (1963).*

The teenage-targeted film *Where the Boys Are* focused on four female students at a midwestern university during spring break. The character Dolores played was Merritt, a freshman in college who, after meeting a handsome college senior also on spring break in Florida, realizes she is not ready for sex. The movie won some awards, inspired many American college students to head to Fort Lauderdale for their annual spring break, and foreshadowed more wise choices by Dolores.

During her next role as Clare in the *Francis of Assisi* movie, Dolores met Pope John XXIII while filming in Rome. Clare was a young woman so inspired by St. Francis that she left her wealthy family and became a nun whom we now call St. Clare of Assisi. After St. Francis recognized Clare as one of those chosen souls destined by God for great things, the future saint set aside her rich dress, cut off her hair, put on a rough tunic, and vowed herself to the service of Jesus Christ.

St. Clare would go on to co-found the religious order now known as the Poor Clares, and the young actress Dolores Hart would add Broadway theater to her growing list of accomplishments as a young actress. In her Broadway debut, Dolores was nominated for a Tony Award in the Best Featured Actress category for her role in *The Pleasure of His Company*.

As the stress of acting and traveling between LA and NYC weighed on Dolores, she took her boyfriend's advice. She found respite at the Abbey of Regina Laudis, a Benedictine monastery in Bethlehem, Connecticut.

The retreat to the Abbey of Regina Laudis gave Dolores the solitude and contemplative atmosphere she needed. She told one of the nuns she was thinking about joining the order, but the Mother of the Abbey told her very directly, "You go back and do your movie thing and get it out of your system."

Dolores returned to Hollywood and continued acting, but she believed God called her to join the Sisters at the Abbey. Her longtime relationship with that boyfriend, architect Don Robinson, complicated her decision. At the end of their first date, Don asked Dolores to marry him, but Dolores asked for some time to just date. He said he would give her all the time she wanted.

They were both Catholic, and Don knew he wanted to marry her as they dated off and on for five years. Though Dolores said she loved him, she did not believe God wanted her to marry him. The breakup devastated her longtime best friend, who had already drawn up designs for their future home, but he supported her. With MGM and 20th Century Fox studios wanting Dolores to sign a seven-year contract worth millions, the up-and-coming actress made a promotional stop in New York for what would be her last film, *Come Fly with Me*.

A month after the film was released, the 24-year-old actress made up her mind to leave the film industry and become a Catholic nun at the Benedictine Abbey of Regina Laudis in Bethlehem, Connecticut. After the promotional stop, Dolores took a one-way car ride to the abbey from New York and never looked back.

> "I just knew that this was what God wanted from me. I never felt I was 'walking away from Hollywood.' I felt I was walking into something more significant, and by that, I took Hollywood with me." –Mother Dolores Hart

POWER SISTERS | 79

At the abbey, Dolores soon befriended a fellow novice who, deep down, thought there was no way this actress would stay. After Dolores had her long, beautiful hair cut as customary for novices, she reconsidered her first impression. The abbey was a picturesque, rural, and secluded enclave which also served as a self-sustaining farm, so the life of a novice was not easy and meant:

- Tilling and working the fields
- Caring for the animals
- Ten novices sharing one bathroom
- Singing seven times a day
- Strict rules limiting visitors

Since her vocation was a call of love, Dolores felt at home despite the work and discipline at the abbey. She did not miss the glamorous world of acting since answering the mysterious call she heard from God with the "ear of the heart," as she put it.

> "Listen with the ears of your heart."
> – Saint Benedict

God had given her a new purpose and mission. One of the things she particularly loved about the cloistered life was the capacity it offered for true communion with God. Dolores never felt she was leaving anything behind and described the monastery as a "powerhouse of prayer" where the nuns carried other people's burdens. That empathy for others and the realization that everyone is created for a distinct mission ironically developed in Dolores during her acting career. While learning her characters, including some saints, she began to understand every individual's unique purpose. She carried that understanding into her religious life.

> "I think we all need to walk down that path of self-discovery and truly understand our purpose. And part of doing that is coming together and sharing our experiences, both the joyful and sorrowful ones. And I truly believe it is never too late." –Mother Dolores Hart

After seven years of prayer, farm work on the abbey, and ongoing discernment following the monastic rules written by Saint Benedict in the sixth century, Dolores took her final vows. She would spend the next two decades in relative isolation, happily praying and working alongside her sisters at the abbey.

As she enjoyed the cloistered life, Sister Dolores had minimal contact with outsiders but continued receiving and answering fan mail. She received hundreds of letters from people nationwide seeking guidance on closer relationships with God. Mother Dolores sees that one of her primary roles is to provide hope. She believes that if you can find hope, you might find faith.

One regular visitor was her former fiancée and lifelong friend, Don Robinson. Don would never marry and admitted he still loved her deeply. He visited Mother Dolores every year at the Abbey on Christmas and Easter and once said, "Every love doesn't have to wind up at the altar." He was a true man of faith, and despite being crushed by the news that she was leaving him for the religious life, he eventually understood that she was meant for greater things in this life.

> *"To find God is to find love. To understand God is to understand love."* – Mother Dolores Hart

Sister Dolores was instrumental at the abbey in developing a stronger connection to the community through the arts. Famous Hollywood stars like Paul Newman and Patricia Neal helped support the abbey's open-air theater, which staged an annual summer musical supported by the nuns for the local community.

Around her twenty-fifth year in the monastery, Sister Dolores received permission to resume an active role as a voting member of the Academy of Motion Picture Arts and Sciences. The group's nearly ten thousand members are best known for the Academy Awards, now officially and popularly known as the Oscars. She remains the only Oscar-voting member of the Academy who is a nun.

In 2001, Sister Dolores was named prioress of the monastery and held that office until 2015. Many new novices found in her a liberated woman who made Elvis blush and gave up everything our culture teaches us to revere, like fame and money, for a deeper relationship with God.

In 2006, Mother Dolores left the abbey for Hollywood and Washington D.C. to raise awareness for idiopathic peripheral neuropathy disorder, a neurological disorder that afflicts her and many Americans. She testified at a congressional hearing on the need to research the painful and crippling disease.

In 2012, Mother Dolores's story was the subject of a short HBO film titled *God Is the Bigger Elvis*. The order allowed the filmmakers unprecedented access to their abbey grounds and the cloistered nuns.

The film received an Oscar nomination for Best Documentary (Short Subject) and showed nuns praying and singing at chapel, milking cows, driving tractors, and caring for pigs.

Mother Dolores was granted the rare privilege of traveling outside the cloister to return to Hollywood and walk the red carpet at the Oscars. Her attire stood out on the carpet, and some onlookers thought she was an actor dressed up for a role. Instead, she served as a witness to God's ever presence, even in a place that seemed to have lost its moral compass.

In 2013, Mother Dolores teamed with Richard DeNeut, a lifelong friend and publicist for the Hollywood firm Globe Photos, and authored a book about her life entitled *The Ear of the Heart: An Actress' Journey from Hollywood to Holy Vows*. She was once again allowed to travel for a short time to talk about the book. Sixty years after leaving the movie industry for an abbey that she says was the grace of God that entered her life unexpectedly, her witness continues to inspire.

When asked why young people especially respond to her, she thinks it is because she kissed Elvis. She also believes the film *Elvis*, released in 2022, reignited interest in him and perhaps the young actress who not only made him blush but shared a love for the Bible with him.

Elvis never liked the term "The King of Rock and Roll" since he knew only one true king, our Father in Heaven. Today, when asked about the kiss, Mother Dolores jokes, "How much closer to Heaven can you get?"

Even in a cloistered abbey, Mother Dolores continued to work with true leading men, such as bishops and priests, to share her faith. One leading man, Saint John Paul II, visited her community of contemplative Benedictine women during his visit to the United States.

She encourages everyone to walk down the path of self-discovery and truly understand one's purpose. Part of that is coming together and sharing joyful and sorrowful experiences. As exemplified by her long-time Hollywood friend, Patricia Neal, who became a Catholic on her deathbed, it is never too late.

Patricia Neal, who once graced the cover of *Life* magazine, is now buried at the abbey where her friend Mother Dolores Hart continues to offer prayers and gratitude so everyone can embark on their own personal journeys in this life and discover their calling from God on their way to eternal life.

CHAPTER CHALLENGE

FAITH CHALLENGE

- Learn more about your Catholic faith through movies and documentaries. Since reading can damage your ignorance, take a break, and enjoy a good film or show for the soul. Invite a friend and introduce them to your faith. Here is a link to start your journey.

WORKS CHALLENGE

- Discover how you can share your faith with others through your talents as an actor, athlete, musician, or scholar. Although many public places limit prayers and faith-based events, the best and most natural way to share your faith is one-on-one with a friend.

CHAPTER 7

SISTER JOSEPHINE GARRETT, CSFN

POWER BAPTIST CONVERT AND UNRULY SPEAKER

"I believe that the most powerful gospel we will ever preach is how we live our daily lives." – Sr. Josephine Garrett

Before she was Sister Josephine, Toni Garrett loved soccer as much as her Baptist faith. Born and raised in Houston, Texas, by her loving and devout Christian aunt and uncle, she was ten years old when the US Women's National soccer team won the first World Cup in 1991, motivating her to improve her skills on the pitch.

Her passion for God and her faith closely matched her speed and energy on the pitch. Even if it meant rushing from a soccer game or practice, Sister Josephine prioritized attending her Baptist services on Wednesdays and Sundays. The energy of the predominantly African-American congregation was contagious, and even today, she asks audiences, "Can I get an Amen?!" after telling them about her Christian upbringing.

After working hard in the classroom and starring on her high school soccer team, Ms. Garrett earned a scholarship to play at the University of Dallas (UD). Although just a 4-hour drive from her home, the traditions of the Catholic University seemed very distant from her Baptist roots. It was so different that when she enrolled in 1999, she and her aunt thought it was "a little weird' not knowing it was Catholic until a few weeks into her freshman year.

Fortunately, her soccer teammates and practices felt normal, and with the U.S. women winning their second World Cup that same year, women's soccer was gaining popularity nationwide. Her team had a successful season, going 11-6, but as a freshman, Ms. Garrett saw limited playing time, getting into just 4 of the 17 games. She did net a goal and celebrated with the exuberance she learned at her Baptist parish while praising the Lord appropriately.

She also found a new group as she focused on her studies during the offseason. Having loved singing in her Baptist church, Ms. Garrett joined the UD Latin liturgical choir to continue her passion for singing His praise. Ms. Garrett learned more about the Catholic Mass as her instructors interpreted these Latin songs.

After a tearful departure from the soccer team, she participated in UD's semester in Rome program. There, she encountered Pope Saint John Paul II several times. As a Baptist girl, she saw in him an amazing preacher. She was clueless about so much happening around her, but she knew he spoke about the God she was taught to love as a child. Yet she felt he was saying so much more.

She relished the opportunity to study Paul's letters to the Corinthians in Corinth and read about the death of Socrates, where scholars believed he died. The experience in Rome was transformational and enhanced her knowledge of the Catholic faith.

She graduated in 2004, completing her bachelor's in arts in political philosophy with a business concentration, and subsequently entered the banking industry. She loved and respected the Catholic Church but did not yet consider conversion from her Baptist roots. She simply didn't see other black Americans in the Catholic Church. So, she was hesitant.

During those early years after college, a nun came to her place of work at the bank and would chat with her. She asked her why she was not Catholic. She mentioned the feeling of being a minority, and the nun introduced her to a black woman who was the RCIA director at a local parish.

Ms. Garrett soon converted and became a regular Sunday churchgoing Catholic with no intentions of joining a religious order. Her focus was on her career.

After an operations and project manager role with 200 direct reports, Ms. Garrett became a Vice President in Bank of America's Home Loans Division.

What drew her to Catholicism?

- The Mass centered on the Eucharist, not on the pastor's personality or the choir's strength.
- This faith was consistent as outlined in the *Catechism*.
- The priests were humble and lived simply compared to some Baptist ministers.

A few years after converting, she had another opportunity to return to Rome with the UD Latin choir. While there, she made what she describes as a significant confession. She started to discern what God made her for and felt the call to consider a religious vocation.

She served as a self-proclaimed "wingman" on a retreat for a friend who was sure she wanted to be a sister. The pair went to the Sisters of the Holy Family of Nazareth convent for a week. Ironically, that friend did not discern a religious vocation, and Sister Josephine served as her maid of honor at her wedding just 15 months later!

After two years of discernment and ten years of climbing the corporate ladder, the former wingman and soccer star entered the Sisters of the Holy Family of Nazareth.

> *"God, we are not doing Sister Act 3."*
> Sister Josephine Jesus, when hearing the call to a religious order.

In 2011, Sister Josephine began her formation to be a religious sister, and in 2020, Sister Josephine professed her final vows as a Sister of the Holy Family of Nazareth. Her family had celebrated her conversion to Catholicism and loved that she loved the Lord, but some thought joining a religious order was too much.

Her middle brother, Andre, said, "You are a cute person. You don't have to do that," referring to her new celibate life. Her brother, Chris, appreciated her vow but felt uncomfortable in the convent. He thought he might "burst into flames" when he walked into the convent to visit her. Her aunt, who raised her Baptist, had been a Catholic of the Dominican order in the Caribbean. She would pray her rosaries and novenas when they would volunteer at hospitals. Her aunt returned to the Catholic faith and attended Mass regularly with Sister Josephine. Her uncle took a little more time to get used to the idea, but he now loves her love for Jesus.

> "Behold, I am the handmaid of the Lord. May it be done to me according to your word."
> Luke 1:38

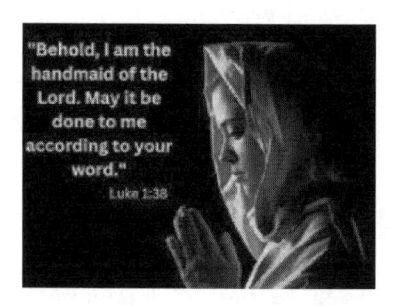

As a Baptist, Sister Josephine did not learn much about Mary, the mother of our Savior Jesus. Once she became a Catholic, she developed a strong devotion to Mary and often turned to her for guidance.

> *"When we give our yes, we don't go it alone."*
> – Sr. Josephine Garrett

On a six-day retreat, she was invited by a Jesuit priest to put herself at the annunciation scene. "Behold, I am the handmaid of the Lord; let it be unto me according to your word." Sister declared she would have turned to Mary and said, "Mary, do you know what you just said yes to, girl?!"

Most of us want a more precise picture before we say "yes" to something. Sister Josephine asked in prayer, "Mary, why do you love Him that much?" To behold means to hold thoroughly to who God says we are; therefore, Mary's response makes more sense. Holding thoroughly gives us the reason and courage to follow Him almost blindly.

She concluded that she would have had to say "yes" because God made her- a simple but profound conclusion.

She points out other Bible verses with "behold," providing an emphatic message.

- Genesis 1:31 And God saw everything that he had made, and **behold**, it was very good.
- Isaiah 12:2 **Behold**, God is my salvation. I will trust and not be afraid.
- Psalm 127:3 **Behold** children are a heritage from the Lord, the fruit of the womb reward.
- Luke 17:25 For **behold,** the kingdom of God is among you.
- John 19:26 On the cross, Jesus said to his mother Woman, **behold** your son. Then He said to his disciple [John] Behold your mother.

The disciple John took Mary into his own home, showing that when we give our yes, we don't go it alone.

Once part of the Holy Family of Nazareth convent, Sister Josephine's contagious laugh, clear love for the Lord, and gregarious personality melded well with her new family of sisters. Their shared passion for Christ and their order's mission outweighed any difference in skin color or background, and they formed a close-knit family.

She shares, "There is not one personality type that fits the mode of a sister or nun. Religious sisters can be gritty and have all kinds of personalities. We go bowling, see movies, and have fun together. We are like a family."

> "The most important name you choose is 'Sister,' not the new name."– Sister Josephine

The Sisters of the Holy Family of Nazareth (CSFN) is an international congregation of vowed religious women dedicated to spreading the Kingdom of God's love, particularly within families. They serve families through active ministry in schools, hospitals, parishes, prisons, and social service agencies. They also spread the Kingdom through their daily living in a community of prayer and commitment to God and the Holy Family.

Today, 1,100 sisters of Nazareth live this vision while serving in 14 countries: Australia, Belarus, England, France, Ghana, Israel, Italy, Kazakhstan, Philippines, Poland, Russia, Spain, Ukraine, and the United States. They are joined by 700 lay associates.

Under the direction of the CSFN General Administration in Rome, the Sisters in these areas dedicate themselves to spreading the kingdom of God's love. The U.S. province of the Sisters of the Holy Family of Nazareth has some 200 sisters serving in Connecticut, Illinois, New York, Ohio, Pennsylvania, and Texas. The Provincialate is in Des Plaines, IL, a Chicago suburb.

Late in her discernment to join a religious order, she also felt the call to become a counselor despite having no formal training in it. She could help someone with budgets and banking, but she didn't quite understand why God called her to help others with their mental health.

> *"Catholic feminism needs to strengthen a woman's sense of self so that she can be a gift and unity can be brought about."*
> –Sister Josephine

Yet, she jumped into her therapy training feet first and learned quickly. As part of the secular training, she and other students had to pick an organization that gave them the most angst. Many of her classmates ironically chose the Catholic Church. She chose feminists and attended a meeting in her habit. The experience opened her eyes to some of the good things feminism promotes and served as an example of how we can move out of our comfort zones to meet people when we evangelize.

> *"I think women have a deep incarnational sense.*
> *There's a natural unruliness to life."*
> – Sister Josephine

She draws strength from Pope Francis's 2013 apostolic exhortation, *The Joy of the Gospel*, when discussing her call to evangelize as a woman. She particularly likes the section where he talks about the "unruly word of God." She cites the call to plant seeds; they will grow while we sleep, and we need to be okay with that. The full quote from *The Joy of the Gospel* reads:

> *"God's word is unpredictable in its power. The Gospel speaks of a seed which, once sown, grows by itself, even as the farmer sleeps (Mark 4:26-29). The Church must accept this unruly freedom of the word, which accomplishes what it wills in ways that surpass our calculations and ways of thinking."* –Pope Francis

Her counseling work covers children, teens, and adults. She currently serves as the school counselor for St. Gregory Cathedral School in Tyler, TX, and has a private practice.

She holds a master's in clinical mental health counseling from The Chicago School of Professional Psychology. She is a Nationally Certified Counselor and a Licensed Professional Counselor Associate in the State of Texas. She also specializes in trauma treatment and is an EMDR-trained clinician.

EMDR stands for Eye Movement Desensitization and Reprocessing and uses neuroscience to change how one's brain deals with traumatic memories and traumatic stress. It works by helping to reprocess traumatic memories to make them less emotionally intense and overwhelming.

Sister Josephine jokes that she avoids working with younger (Pre-K) children since they scare her, but she does spend much of her time working with families to support children of all ages.

> *"God wants us to be healthy mentally as well as spiritually."* – Sister Josephine

She advocates that the first step a parent should take when a child is struggling is to "open a door to a discussion" with the child. Later steps include finding an advocate who can speak to the parents on behalf of the child. The advocate could be a teacher, youth minister, or coach who interacts with the child. Parents must accept some discomfort to properly deal with a child's mental health issues.

She believes the number one thing teens need is a meaningful connection. That's not a connection to a strong Wi-Fi signal but a connection to other humans. She uses the example of when two people stand face to face, and one rubs her own hands together to warm them up. The person observing feels her hands warming up as well—the neurons in the human brain work in an amazing way.

She also encourages parents and her student patients to not strive for perfection but to strive for instead a willingness to repair. The advice works well for Christians. God knows we are not perfect, but he wants us to repent, and fortunately, the Catholic Church provides the powerful sacrament of confession for a start to repair.

> *"I wouldn't strive for perfection, but I encourage others to strive for a willingness to repair."*
> – Sister Josephine Garrett

When she sees a patient's or parent's progress, she cheers them on with pom poms. Yes, she literally has pom poms in her office and pulls them out when appropriate.

She has become very active on social media since joining her order's vocational committee. As a spouse of Christ, she feels a call to serve as a public intercessor. She's sometimes reluctant to post or respond on social media, but she knows she must do so for Him. So, she pauses and prays before sharing on social media. What a great lesson for all.

When out, people will often ask her, "Are you real?" They think she may be in costume since she does not look like a "typical" nun. But she does look like the 13" Sr. Mary Clara doll, which pays tribute to the many holy religious sisters serving God worldwide. The doll has a 16-page companion booklet featuring five true vocational stories highlighting selflessness, hard work, charity, and courage. It's written to help parents foster vocations within the family.

Sister Josephine also serves in the vocations ministry and as a national speaker for youth and young adults, speaking to groups of up to 25,000 at various Catholic conferences.

> "I think sometimes people think that by the vow of celibacy, I have closed myself off, but I've actually opened myself to the entire world, and so, I am not for one, so that I can be for all."
> – Sr. Josephine Garrett

Once, a young woman asked her what living celibate is like. Sr. Josephine said, "It is wild," and laughingly shared how wonderful her family of sisters is. She especially enjoys her Nazareth community since it does not focus on only one type of apostolate. Instead, each sister's gifts can be put at the service of the present needs of the Church. Becoming a Nazareth Sister was the 2nd greatest surprise that God had in mind for her. The 1st was becoming Catholic.

She believes we taste home in each reception of the Eucharist, and our longing and identification with hope grows with each reception of the Eucharist. But we are pilgrims; we are prophets proclaiming the Kingdom of Love and the call to be one family in God. That's our journey until all are reconciled in Christ.

Sr. Josephine loves to read and shares her favorite authors.

1. *Father Jacques Philippe* -- a member of the community of the Beatitudes in France who writes about prayer, interior freedom, and peace of heart, selling millions of books worldwide.

2. *Renee Brown* -- an American professor, podcast host, and author of six NY Times best-selling books in her field of social work and psychology.

She also listens to Power Priests' Fr. Mike Schmitz's Bible in a Year podcast regularly since she loves the Bible. She recently authored her own book, *Hope: An Invitation*.

In the book, Sr. Josephine invites readers to journey with her to a new depth of hope, to discover the courage to press ahead into the unknown even in difficult and seemingly impossible circumstances. She shares her own struggles to live in hope despite challenging circumstances in her own life, and she reflects on the significant problem and the great gift of hope. Ultimately, we must find our hope in the strength of the Lord since we need a hope that extends well beyond ourselves and into eternity -- a hope that comes from God, who not only has given us hope but allows us to spread this hope to others.

CHAPTER CHALLENGE

FAITH CHALLENGE

- Learn the Act of Contrition and find time for a thorough confession to restore your relationship with God.

O my God, I am heartily sorry for having offended Thee, and I detest all my sins because of Thy just punishments, but most of all, because they offend Thee, my God, Who are all-good and deserving of all my love.
I firmly resolve, with the help of Thy grace, to sin no more and to avoid in the near occasion of sin. Amen.

> "Struggles don't mean the relationship is over. We can be restored."
> – Sr. Josephine Garrett

WORKS CHALLENGE

- Check out Sister Josephine's course, *Mental Health in Parish Ministry*, released by Revive. Mental Health concerns are prevalent, with 1 in 5 adults experiencing mental health concerns and 1 in 6 teens reporting a major depressive episode in 2020. Advocate for someone in need, and if they show the following three signs, encourage them to seek counseling.

    1. Long frequency and/or duration
    2. High severity or excessive tearfulness
    3. Creating distress in their daily life

CHAPTER 8

SISTER M. THERESE ANTONE, RSM, ED.D

POWER UNIVERSITY PRESIDENT AND CHANCELLOR

"May you travel the path of life in peace with faith as compass and love as your Lonestar." – Sr. Therese Antone

In the state of Rhode Island, Catholics were once forbidden by law to hold public office or even vote. Over the past three decades, a Sister of Mercy has led Salve Regina University in Newport, Rhode Island, as President and Chancellor.

Armed with a Doctor of Education degree from Harvard University, Sister M. Therese Antone, RSM, Ed. D, served as President of Salve Regina from 1994-2009 and Chancellor since.

Under Sister Antone's leadership, Salve Regina's national rankings and student profile rose, and its endowment grew from $1 million to $40 million. The university spent $76 million on renovations and expansion and received numerous awards for restoring the historic mansions, cottages, and gatehouses on the 80-acre oceanside campus.

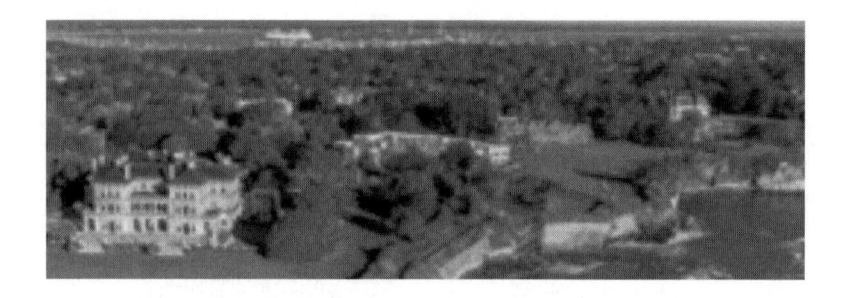

Salve Regina University is located alongside mansions built as summer cottages by leaders of finance and industry during the Gilded Age of the late 19th century. With stunning ocean views and these historic homes as neighbors, it is not your average campus, and Dr. Therese Antone, RSM, is not your average religious sister.

Born in Central Falls, a suburb of Providence, RI, Therese was the third of seven children raised in Cumberland, RI, by Florence Smith Antone and George P. Antone, a cobbler. When her dad was not repairing shoes, he was a communicant and member of the Knights of Columbus at their Catholic parish, St. Aidan.

Her mother, Florence, was a voracious reader who stayed home and ensured faith and education were a priority for all their children. Later in life, she would continue to share her Catholic faith as a grandmother of twenty-one and great-grandmother to sixteen.

Therese's childhood was simple but fun. Her two older brothers fed her competitive spirit, and she enjoyed riding bikes, hiking the hills near their home, and playing school. Her dad encouraged her to be a teacher since she always played the teacher as a child. The seeds for a career in education were planted early.

During her senior year at Cumberland High School, Therese met a Sister of Mercy who inspired her to join the order and later attend Salve Regina, when it was an all-girls college run by the Sisters of Mercy.

Though Rhode Island denied voting rights to Catholics from 1719 to 1783, the state granted a charter to the Sisters of Mercy for Salve Regina in 1934. The charter wanted the school to "promote virtue, and piety and learning" but left open all educational options to the sisters, who wanted to teach men as well as women.

After more than a dozen years of careful preparation, one of those Gilded Age mansions was gifted to the college, enabling Salve Regina to welcome its first class of fifty-eight women. That was in the fall of 1947, two years after the end of the Second World War, when many involved in the war effort were returning to college.

Inspired by Catherine McAuley, who founded the order in 1831 in Dublin, Ireland, the Sisters of Mercy kept education at the heart of their effort.

That focus prompted the sisters to expand the college to include male students in 1973 and attain university status in 1991. Three years later, Sr. Therese would infuse her energy as president.

That educational focus also inspired Therese Antone to join the order and continue her academic journey with advanced degrees. While serving in her active ministry, Sister Therese went on to get a master's degree from Villanova University and then a Doctor of Education degree from Harvard University. She also completed the senior executive program at the MIT Sloan School of Management while serving as Executive Vice-President of Salve Regina.

The degrees made her parents proud and would have impressed the order's founder, Catherine McAuley, who sought, through her service to the poor, sick, and uneducated, to reveal the mercy of God in our world.

With a particular concern for women, Sister Catherine McAuley endeavored to help them recognize their inherent dignity and become self-directing and self-sustaining at a time when opportunities for them were limited. Education was at the heart of her efforts.

Academic excellence was also at the heart of Sister Therese's efforts at Salve Regina University, as indicated by her message to the university, which stayed true to her founder's initial mission and vision.

> "Sustained by the enduring vision of the Sisters of Mercy, Salve Regina's growth as a Catholic university has been nourished by highly qualified faculty and staff dedicated to the mission. Their generosity and friendship are both an inspiration and the foundation for continuing our history of excellence in the Mercy tradition."
> – Sister M. Therese Antone

On the campus, students are reminded of that Mercy tradition by a statue of Sister Catherine McAuley, whose story is worthy of a chapter of its own, but just a condensed version follows. Every year around Mercy Day on September 24, they remember her life on campus with a week-long celebration.

Born in Dublin, Ireland, in 1778, Catherine had a modest upbringing. In 1824, she used her inheritance from an Irish couple she had served for twenty years to build a large house of mercy. There, she, and other laywomen would shelter homeless women, reach out to the sick and dying, and educate poor girls. Catherine also cared for nine children, which included five from her deceased sister and four adopted orphans.

To give these efforts greater stability, Catherine and her co-workers founded a new religious congregation in 1831 despite some opposition from some local bishops who questioned the need for a new religious order. Now known as Sister Mary Catherine, the founder traveled throughout Ireland and England, opening convents and houses of mercy to expand their services.

In 1841, Pope Gregory XVI formally confirmed the Sisters of Mercy just a few months before the founder's death. Two years later, the Sisters came to the United States to establish hospitals, orphanages, and schools.

For nearly two centuries, the Sisters of Mercy have maintained a presence worldwide and have been deeply involved in education, health care, pastoral ministry, and social services. Their network includes universities, secondary and elementary

POWER SISTERS | 103

schools, and one of the largest U.S. health systems that covers five midwestern states. All focus on these core values:

1. Spirituality
2. Community
3. Service
4. Social Justice and Our Critical Concerns
5. Works of Mercy

In 1990, Pope John Paul II declared Catherine McAuley Venerable, recognizing her profound charity and faith.

> *"The spiritual and corporal works of mercy which draw religious from a life of contemplation, so far from separating them from the love of God, unite them more closely to Him and render them more valuable in His holy service."*
> – The Venerable Catherine McAuley

Inspired by the core values and focus on both spiritual and corporal works of mercy (see faith challenge), one Salve Regina graduate continued to promote the founder's global expansion and message of mercy.

True to her father's prognostication, Sister Therese's career included teaching at all levels. She served as principal of a coeducational secondary school and Director of Finance for Sisters of Mercy, serving in Rhode Island and Central America.

In her finance role, the math teacher learned a lasting lesson about fundraising. A member of the Dana Foundation, a large philanthropic organization in New York City, told her during a lunch meeting that they could not donate due to restrictions but that she should keep doing what she was doing. Keep selling the vision.

Selling the vision of Catherine McAuley, Jesus Christ, and Salve Regina University is how Sister Therese would successfully lead in Rhode Island and worldwide.

Before acceding to Salve Regina University's presidency in 1994, she was a faculty member, the Director of Development, Vice President/Institutional Advancement, and the Executive Vice President for Corporate Affairs and Advancement.

In just her second year as president, Sister Therese was instrumental in pushing Congress to establish the Pell Center for International Relations and Public Policy at Salve Regina, bringing high-profile leaders to the campus and enhancing the university's reputation.

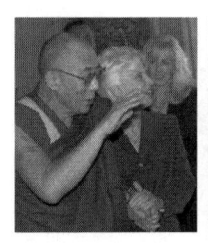

One of those high-profile leaders was the Dalai Lama, who visited the school in 2005 to speak about a human approach to world peace. The foremost spiritual leader of Tibetan Buddhism discussed religious life with Sister Therese, who recalls the meeting as one of her most moving experiences ever. His analogy for their respective lives as religious leaders was like a lotus flower that thrives in dirty water but carries no dirt inside it. All Christians can heed this advice when trying to live the faith in a world that en masse rejects it.

Sister Therese's global focus did not stop with establishing the Pell Center at Salve Regina. She has worked with Maronite priests at a Catholic university in Lebanon for thirteen years and Mercy sisters in Tanzania, Belize, Kenya, and Syria. Just as the Pell Center was designed to help students not just study the world but to change it, Sister Therese has spread Jesus Christ's message of mercy, love, and forgiveness globally.

> *"You shall love the Lord your God with all your heart and with all your soul and with all your mind. This is the greatest and first commandment. The second is like it: You shall love your neighbor as yourself."* – Matthew 22:37-40

Closer to home, Sister Therese served and continues to serve on many boards and committees. Some include:

- Defense Advisory Committee for Women in the Military
- Commission on Women in Higher Education
- Rhode Island State Ethics Commission
- Board of Directors of the National Association of Independent Colleges and Universities (NAICU)
- Board of Directors of Global Net Lease
- Board of Trustees – Bank Newport
- Board of Advisors – Fleet Bank
- Board of Advisors – U.S. Naval War College
- Board of Governors of Newport Health Care Corp.
- The Finance Council of the Diocese of Providence

The mix of educational, government, Catholic, and finance boards demonstrates her skills and knowledge diversity. She credits her dad, who invested wisely as a cobbler to provide for his large family, as the root of her financial acumen. As busy as these roles keep her, Sister Therese never forgets that people are the focus of her ministry as it was for Christ. She has never been above helping with renovations or serving meals to those in need.

Even as the recipient of many awards, including the National Conference Humanitarian Award, the Mercy Higher Education Leadership Award, and the John E. Fogarty Achievement Award, Sister Therese is quick to acknowledge how many wonderful and well-qualified faculty, staff, and administrators assisted her in her mission. She loves to spend time with them and students on campus, in church, and on the golf course.

With the Salve Regina President role in the good hands of Dr. Kelli Armstrong and her right hand, Dr. Nancy Schreiber, Provost and VP of Academic Affairs, Sister Therese has a little more time to socialize and enjoy an occasional round of golf. When she has time and the weather is right, she has been known to find golf partners immediately after morning Mass.

> *"The real meaning of life is to reach out to the other person and help."*
> – Sister Therese

This Rhode Island Heritage Hall of Famer has enjoyed the game for decades since a colleague suggested she take up the game, and that Christmas gave her six free golf lessons and a new club at each class. In her development and leadership roles, she has found the time on the course with donors and friends fruitful.

When not bringing the unique perspective of a religious sister to corporate boards or leading a university, this power sister loves spending time with family. She is regarded as a fun aunt and great aunt to many, and this octogenarian has no plans to slow down any time soon.

> "I am amazed she's a Sister of Mercy. I can see her as a [United States] senator."
> – Nuala Pell, a long-time friend, and wife of Senator Clayborn Pell

Sister Therese can be seen cruising around Newport in her BMW, which she assures she purchased at an excellent price to fit in with the high-quality image she wants to portray for the university. When asked by one board member about the optics, she innocently shared that she could see fine through the windshield.

As chancellor, her message is consistent with her faith and the vows she made as a Sister of Mercy.

> "God is the creator of all things, and we are connected to all things. The message of Jesus Christ was of love and forgiveness, and I remind students to be more respectful and listen to understand each other. We should never forget the contributors from the past, but realize we are responsible for the future."

CHAPTER CHALLENGE

FAITH CHALLENGE

- Learn the Spiritual and Corporal Works of Mercy.

THE SPIRITUAL WORKS	THE CORPORAL WORKS
Instruct the ignorant	Feed the hungry
Counsel the doubtful	Give drink to the thirsty
Admonish the sinner	Clothe the naked
Bear wrongs patiently	Welcome the stranger
Forgive offenses willingly	Visit the sick
Comfort the afflicted	Visit the imprisoned
Pray for the living and the dead	Bury the dead
Grateful contemplation of God's world	Care for our common home

WORKS CHALLENGE

- Put into action these works of mercy regularly. It can be as simple as donating clothing to a shelter or volunteering at a food kitchen.

POWER SISTERS | 109

CHAPTER 9

SISTER MARIS STELLA KARALEKAS SV

POWER NAVAL SISTER FOR LIFE

> *"If we're willing to give up our lives for our country, surely giving your life to God is something even more noble. He's a worthy cause."* – Sister Maris Stella

Sister Maris Stella began her military career at the most selective of the service academies, the U.S. Naval Academy in Annapolis, Maryland. In high school, she felt the need to do something significant and meaningful with her life, and the academy was a terrific opportunity for a free education and to serve her country.

She was pleasantly surprised to get selected since the Naval Academy only accepted roughly eight percent of applicants, but her life-changing experiences there were an even bigger surprise. Surrounded by students and faculty with a great attitude of service, sacrifice, and a love for God, she encountered virtue formation first-hand.

"Part of the experience is being formed in some of the natural virtues of sacrifice and service," she said. "We would go around in our uniforms, and people would thank us for our service, but we really knew we were serving something greater than ourselves."

The desire to serve something greater stuck with her during and after her college years. In her second year at the academy, she embarked on a Holy Land pilgrimage, where she experienced a significant moment in her life. She visited the Garden of Gethsemane at the foot of the Mount of Olives in Jerusalem, where Jesus Christ underwent the agony in the garden and was arrested before his crucifixion. While sitting in the garden, she looked up and saw a religious sister walk by in a habit.

Her presence awakened something in the midshipman. Sister Maris Stella later explained, "She was really saying with her life what was in my heart: this desire to give myself not just for something greater, but really for someone, to give my whole life to God."

Before she could give her whole life to God, she had two more years of the academy and a five-year service commitment following graduation. She relished seeing what the world had to offer and formed lifetime friendships. At the academy, she was involved in various sports and joined the triathlon team to represent her school and focus on her fitness in swimming, cycling, and running. Little did she know the training was seemingly becoming a pre-requisite for religious sisters (see chapter 11 on Sister Madonna Bruder).

After graduation and her commissioning, Sister Maris Stella served on active duty for five years as a surface warfare officer. As a newly commissioned officer, her service journey began on a naval destroyer as a gunnery officer responsible for the operation and maintenance of the ship's guns and ammunition. During this assignment, she spent hundreds of days off South America's coast pursuing drug traffickers.

Her experience at sea only drew her closer to God. Out at sea, hundreds of miles from shore, she was fascinated by God's creation as she stared at the star-filled sky at night. She was in awe that "God, who made all of this, also made me, and He loves me. He has placed His love in every human person that He's created."

Without access to a Catholic priest or chaplain, as they are called in the military during some deployments, the young Ensign Karalekas served as a Catholic lay leader on the ships. She and her fellow Catholic shipmates would gather for Sunday service and periodic Bible studies to grow their faith while at sea.

After a few years, the Navy assigned her to Naples, Italy, where she served as a liaison officer. In that role, the Lieutenant advised the senior officers on all matters pertaining to U.S. and Italian relations at strategic and operational levels. She also served as a direct representative of the commanding officer to maintain a productive working relationship between the U.S. Navy and Italian military and government officials.

> *"While I was at sea, I came to know God and the beauty of His creation through the men and women with whom I served."*
> – Sister Maris Stella

While stationed in Italy, she was able to visit Rome and the Vatican and witness how young and alive the Catholic Church was. She also got to know some European religious communities and met other young women entering religious life. These religious sisters were bright and talented, and she realized they had a beautiful life. Sisterhood was not some last option for them but a special invitation from God. As she was getting out of the military, she understood that God was offering her this invitation, and she soon decided to follow her love and dedicate her life to serving God.

> *"I served in the Navy, and I tasted many of the good things that this world had to offer, but I knew my heart was made for something more."* –Sister Maris Stella

As a child at Christ the King parish in Ludlow, Massachusetts, Sister Maris Stella already had a strong sense of where her faith journey would take her. The day after her First Communion, she consecrated her life to Jesus through Mary. She credits the Blessed Mother for caring for her whole life and protecting her vocation. Her parents, Peter and Elaine Karalekas, get credit for instilling the faith early in her and her three siblings.

Within a year of finishing her active-duty commitment with the Navy, Sister Maris Stella entered the Sisters of Life convent shortly after attending a discernment retreat with the sisters. She prayed a 33-day novena to Mary and returned to her childhood parish, where she first dedicated herself to Jesus through Mary. That same day, she received her acceptance letter from the Sisters of Life and knew Mary cared for her.

She was amazed by the community's charism (spiritual gift) and focus on the gift of life by helping pregnant women in crisis and through a post-abortion healing mission. When she met the Sisters of Life, she could hardly believe something so unique existed in the Church, and she wanted to be part of their gift to the world since it aligned with what was in her heart.

The late Cardinal John O'Connor founded the Sisters of Life in New York in 1991. Based in the New York area, they are also located in Denver, Philadelphia, Phoenix, Washington, D.C., and Ontario, Canada. The community of Catholic religious women profess four vows:

1. Poverty
2. Chastity
3. Obedience
4. To protect and enhance the sacredness of human life

The navy veteran joined the sisters who dedicate their lives to offering support and resources to pregnant women and mothers, hosting retreats, evangelizing, practicing outreach to college students, and helping women who suffer after abortion.

On the latter, the former gunnery officer's message for women who have had an abortion was simply, "No sin is too great for God's mercy."

Eight years after entering the Sisters of Life, Sister Marie Stella professed her final vows in 2014 in front of her parents, siblings, fellow sisters, and many of her Naval Academy classmates. Her friends from the military, even if they were not Catholic, intuitively understood why she entered religious life. They understood the meaning of sacrifice and that her vows were a "recognition that if we're willing to give up our lives for our country, surely giving your life to God is something even more noble. He's a worthy cause."

The name the former Lieutenant Karalekas chose connected her childhood promise with her naval experience. She chose Sister Maris Stella after our blessed mother, Mary Star of the Sea, who was the shining light that led her to Christ.

While living out her vocation, Sister Maris Stella saw many of her military friends. Many of them supported the sisters' work, especially by helping with their annual Christmas party in New York. They have supported her from the start, and the twelve academy classmates who came to her final vows are incredibly close.

With many of those classmates now married, Sister Maris Stella appreciates their witness to the beauty of Catholic marriage. She

POWER SISTERS | 115

feels being the bride of Christ is the most beautiful gift. She shared, "I'm so grateful for it. I love my vocation."

She also shared a special message with those who are discerning religious life.

> *"It's such a fulfilling, joyful life. God takes nothing away; He gives us everything. While it might appear to be a sacrifice on the front end, we receive a hundredfold."* –Sister Maris Stella

She recommended spending time with Jesus in the Eucharist, where He can tell us the truth and help us discover how He made our hearts to love in this world. He can help us discover why He's created us.

In 2015, Sister Maris Stella moved to Denver, Colorado, with three other sisters to start the group's tenth convent and its first convent in the West. The four women visit college campuses in the area each month to connect with students.

Armed with a master's in theology from the Augustine Institute, she aims to bring hope to young pregnant mothers and heal those grieving an abortion.

Her mission in the military and now as a religious sister paralleled each other as she worked to protect innocent lives and care for those in need. She and her fellow Sisters of Life in Denver fulfill this mission in three ways:

1. Serving pregnant women who live with them at their convent for up to six months after giving birth.
2. Offering post-abortive ministry.
3. Evangelizing on college campuses, specifically to young women.

The sisters know that women in college are vulnerable to abortion because they have their whole lives ahead of them, and sometimes, women who become pregnant think that they won't be able to fulfill their dreams if they have their child. They offer hope on college campuses by providing alternatives for these women.

In her role, Sister Maris Stella sees so many women making heroic choices for life, and she is inspired by those they work with, especially the mothers.

> *"Seeing the sacrifices that moms are willing to make for their children inspires us to make sacrifices for our spiritual children."* – Sister Maris Stella

Sister Maris Stella is amazed, especially by young moms who bring their children to Sunday Mass. She shared, "I think her prayers must be so valuable to the Lord and so precious to God because she is giving all she has to her children, and, in that way, giving it all to God."

The sacrifice these mothers and fathers of young children make parallels the sacrifice of the Mass and is precisely what the Lord wants.

> *"Let the children come to me, and do not hinder them, for such belongs the kingdom of God."*
> – Luke 18:16

For women who have gone through an abortion, Sister Maris Stella emphasized the sisters' hope and healing mission. She considers that mission one of the most beautiful works since many of these women think they cannot be forgiven, and the Sisters remind them that there is no sin too great for God's mercy and that He longs to heal them and restore their faith.

As these women heal and discover the beautiful woman God created, the sisters help them live out that identity rather than anything the culture tells them. After hearing God's word, these women no longer squander the gifts given to them or fall into traps that the culture has set for them.

> *"All life is good; life is sacred, and each person we encounter is a masterpiece of God's love."* –Sister Stella

By helping mothers and their children, Sister Maris Stella is joyfully fulfilling her high school goal and doing something great and meaningful with her life.

CHAPTER CHALLENGE

FAITH CHALLENGE

- Sister Maris Stella developed a close relationship with Mary through prayer. Pray the rosary today and every day as Mary asked of us. If you think it's repetitive, follow the mysteries daily to recall the significant events of Christ's time on earth and pray for someone on each bead.

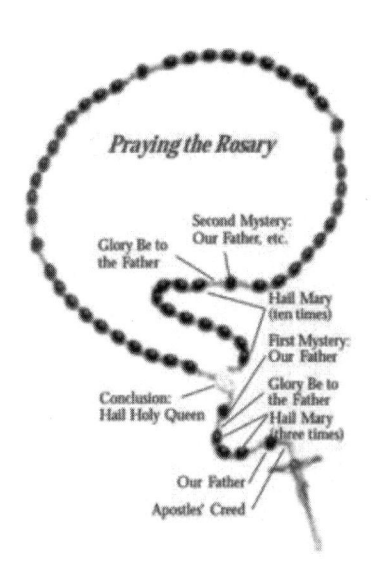

WORKS CHALLENGE

- Just as Sister Maris Stella and her Sisters of Life support college students, consider how you can support FOCUS ministries on college campuses. FOCUS stands for Fellowship of Catholic University Students and is an outreach program for American college students. Learn more at https://focus.org/

CHAPTER 10

SISTER ALICIA TORRES F.E.
POWER RUNNER & CHEF

"The Eucharist is my strength."
– Sister Alicia Torres

Leanne and Manuel Torres always knew their oldest daughter, Alicia, had the conscience to become a nun. She was home-schooled with a Catholic elementary curriculum and enrolled in a Catholic high school in Massachusetts, where several religious sisters and brothers inspired her. However, she had no intention of following in their footsteps.

Alicia regularly attended daily Mass with her mother and siblings and constantly engaged her mother in intense spiritual conversations. Her father would join them at Mass when the demands of his naval career allowed him, and he shared, "I thought that sooner or later she would be religious. I suspected that for years. I knew she wanted to try to help the needy and promote the [Catholic] faith."

When Alicia entered Loyola of Chicago for college, she initially planned to follow in her dad's footsteps and join the Navy. She focused her studies on theology and bioethics, determined to become a naval officer and achieve justice for women in the military. She wanted to become a change agent, but God would guide her along a new path.

Her eyes and heart also sought justice for those impacted by the abortion industry. She saw abortion as one of the greatest injustices against women and children and, in high school and college, was active in the pro-life movement.

- Praying at abortion clinics and opening her apartment to women in crisis pregnancies
- Lobbying at the state capitol in Springfield, Illinois
- Marching in Washington, D.C.

During her sophomore year at Loyola University, something started to turn in her heart when the campus culture sadly became more accepting of abortion. She felt at a loss because she felt her efforts were failing. She turned to prayer and specifically spending time in Eucharistic adoration. That precious time led her to form an actual personal relationship with Jesus. The Eucharist became more real, transforming her intellectual faith into heart-felt transformational faith.

As part of her transformational faith, Alicia started focusing more on people rather than systems. She was an independent

> *"I finally met Jesus after being Catholic my whole life."* – Sister Alicia Torres

young lady with big goals. While her friends were taking the train to serve at a soup kitchen in downtown Chicago, she focused on what she thought were more significant issues. She had not focused much on poverty or feeding the hungry until God revealed the call to her. His calls did not end there.

Alicia began to sense an invitation as the Mass became more real.

She and a close guy friend were similarly ambitious and growing in their faith. They would frequent their favorite college bar specializing in Belgian beers, discuss how to change the world, and then go to Eucharistic adoration. Sitting in silence in front of the real presence of Christ, Alicia felt something in her heart. Jesus was asking her to become a religious sister.

Perhaps due to the drinks before adoration or just the usual human hesitation, Alicia had a long and hard-fought battle with Jesus for a couple of years after that invitation. With plans for a naval career out the window, Alicia changed her major to English and eventually accepted the invite, but that was not the only shocker He had in store for her. With years of pro-life focus, she assumed she would join a religious community that cared for women and children in need and would help end abortion. The community to which Jesus led her was focused on caring for the poor, and she did not fight Him since she knew through prayer it was right.

As part of the call, she felt God wanted her to know people, love people and serve people. He wanted her to give her life to specific people who had hearts, souls, and stories. He wanted her to see Him and love Him in every person.

> *"Amen, I say to you, whatever you did for one of the least of these least brothers of mine, you did for me."*
> – Matthew 25:40

During her discernment, Alicia visited some Franciscan Sisters near the Shrine of Our Lady of Knock in Ireland. These wonderful and holy sisters welcomed Alicia and shared with her some insights into their community as well as the beautiful story behind the nearby shrine, a popular pilgrimage site. In 1879, the Blessed Virgin

Mary appeared with Saint Joseph, Saint John the Evangelist, angels, and Jesus Christ (the Lamb of God).

Invigorated by her visit and armed with her degree from Loyola University Chicago, Alicia was ready to answer God's call, but one more obstacle stood in her way. She also could not formally join the Franciscans of the Eucharist right away because she was carrying $94,000 in student debt that had to be repaid before she could take a vow of poverty. Although her hobbies included reading, stargazing, coffee, falcons, and the Middle Ages, she decided to raise money by running the Chicago Half Marathon.

> *"If God wants you to do something, he clears the way."*
> – Sister Alicia Torres

She had never been a runner, but to enter the convent, she was willing to learn. Her efforts soon received national publicity, and after the half-marathon and several more runs along with the help of the Labouré Society, her debt was down to $12,000. An anonymous donor paid the final balance. Upon hearing this, Alicia shared, "That's a sign not just for me, but for the community."

After finishing the half marathon, she transformed her training into a running club for neighborhood youth and dreamt of the day she would lead a 5K wearing her habit.

Once debt-free, Alicia started running down the path she heard God calling her to follow. Though she encountered romantic possibilities that tested her resolve, she was clearly on the right path. It led her to Father Bob Lombardo, a Franciscan priest who told her about a small group of men and women discerning religious life at the mission where he served. They were the beginnings of the Franciscans of the Eucharist of Chicago, and Alicia found their simple life of prayer and service suited her well.

The Franciscans of the Eucharist live among and serve the poor in Chicago's West Humboldt Park neighborhood. Their life centers upon their relationship with Jesus Christ in the Eucharist. They emphasize encounters with Jesus in the Eucharist both at Mass and in Eucharistic Adoration and believe that if one cannot see Jesus in the Eucharist, one cannot see Him in the poor. Out of their life of prayer flows their community life and three apostolates:

1. Service to the poor
2. Evangelization
3. Teaching

Her journey came full circle after completing her years of religious formation and her master's degree in teaching from Dominican University in River Forest. Alicia and Sister Kate O'Leary professed final vows with the religious order. Scan the QR code for a brief video of the touching ceremony.

> *"There's a tremendous relationship between our Lord's true presence in the Eucharist and His presence to His people, especially those who are suffering and in need."*
> – Sister Alicia Torres

POWER SISTERS | 125

After professing her final vows, Sister Alicia continued working as a religion teacher in an inner-city Catholic school in Chicago, helping feed over four hundred families at their weekly food pantry. She also became involved in many media projects and contributed articles to several online and print outlets, including *First Things, Catholic News Service, America Magazine,* and *Living City.* She would soon bring national attention to the challenges of feeding the hungry when she appeared on the Food Network's popular cooking program, *Chopped,* in 2015.

At age thirty, Sister Alicia was the youngest of the four chefs invited for a special edition of *Chopped* featuring volunteers from different food kitchens nationwide. Each contestant was tasked with using typical makings of a conventional Thanksgiving dinner on the show. The cooks' four ingredients were turkey, green beans, potatoes, and cranberries.

In the appetizer round, Sister Alicia transformed leftovers into Mexican-style quesadillas. She made a Mediterranean-style dish for the entree with curry turkey, sweet potato cranberry hash, and a dipping sauce with goat cheese and green beans. When the other finalist failed to get his side dish of potatoes on the plate for the judges, Sister Alicia became the *Chopped* champion, winning $10,000 for Our Lady of the Angels Mission to provide more home-cooked meals for those in need.

"The Lord gave me this talent," Sister Alicia told the show's judges, who ribbed her for harboring some secret culinary training. "I believe the kitchen is my canvas where I get to express myself creatively."

According to her fellow sisters, Sister Alicia became a minor celebrity after being on national television and winning the competition. Still, she has not let the fame get to her head. She prayed that her newfound fame would bring some attention to the issue of hunger.

"God can take this little nun from Chicago who never went to culinary school to compete. Nothing is impossible with God." – Sister Alicia

In Chicago, after her story landed on the front page of The Chicago Tribune, Sister Alicia often felt as if she was walking around the city with a sign hanging around her neck. People would approach her and ask, "Are you the nun who won *Chopped*?" She was charmed by those encounters, but deeper down, an inner friction left her unsettled. Her vocation was about serving others and a far deeper encounter than a TV show about food. Years later, she discovered the most profound manifestations of this encounter through her students.

One of her special needs students was very non-verbal. She asked him to draw a picture of Jesus two months after their lesson on the Eucharist. He drew a circle with a cross in the middle of it. When she asked him about it, he kept repeating "God, God" and pointing to the host he had drawn.

During the COVID-19 pandemic, Sister Alicia wanted to offer something to ease some anxious students and ground them in their faith. She led the entire school, kindergartners through eighth grade (both in-person and online students), in a modified version of St. Ignatius' Spiritual Exercises. The main point was simple: to come to know, love, and serve Jesus by letting Jesus know, love, and serve us.

As they made the adventure through the Spiritual Exercises, she saw the children's love and devotion for Jesus deepen. The youngest children were captivated by the mystery of the Eucharist. In some of their drawings, they would even write "Jesus" in the host to remember it is really He.

As she saw their love for the Eucharist kindled, she wanted to share the deep friendship she felt with Jesus during her daily holy hour that she had made for over a decade. She led a virtual adoration by connecting to a live stream from the Cathedral of the Good Shepherd in Singapore.

Through technology, her students joined the people in that cathedral so far away for quiet time with Jesus. She had the children sit or kneel in silence, talk to Jesus from their hearts, and let him speak to them. She felt grace in the room and more like a disciple among disciples than a teacher among students as they remained silent for five minutes.

One of the boys placed his hands over his heart as he exclaimed, "My heart was on fire!" Many children said they wanted to tell Jesus, "I love you."

Soon after this experience, Sr Alicia's Eucharistic adoration mission went national through the United States Bishops' Conference initiative. After her assignment to the executive committee as co-coordinator with the priests who would become National Eucharistic Preachers, she helped organize a retreat for priests in Chicago in 2022. The event preceded the Catholic church's National Eucharistic Revival, a three-year initiative by the U.S. bishops that aims to inspire, educate, and unite the faithful in a more intimate relationship with Jesus in the Eucharist.

The revival launched on June 19, 2022, coinciding with the Feast of Corpus Christi, and will close with a National Eucharistic Congress on the Feast of Corpus Christi in 2024. Sister Alicia has enjoyed seeing the priests embrace the renewal of their priestly vocation after she shared the mission and more information about the revival.

> *"Priests have a critical role in bringing the people to the Eucharist and the Eucharist to the people."*
> – Sister Alicia Torres

Sister Alicia has also rediscovered her role in the Church by supporting something so essential. As a member of the Franciscans of the Eucharist, the connection between St. Francis of Assisi and the Eucharist is not lost on her. She shared, "So many people do not realize how Eucharistic Saint Francis of Assisi was. He wrote a letter to every priest in the entire world after Lateran IV emphasizing putting into practice what the [13th century] Council called for around respect and reverence of the Eucharist."

When she is not helping lead a national revival, Sister Alicia and her fellow sisters continue their mission to the poor on the west side of Chicago. She cannot imagine living any other way, even when she hears gunshots almost every day, just like the people who live in her neighborhood. She is not afraid because she believes the Lord asked her, and he is intimately united with her and the source of her strength.

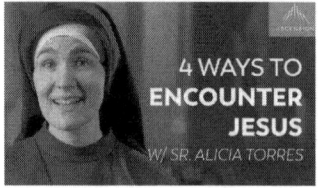

This power sister and "mother to many children" in her classroom literally ran (13.1 miles) to heed the call of Pope Benedict XVI when he bid his young flock to consider religious life. She continues to answer the call daily and draws strength for her journey through the Eucharist as she teaches, cooks, and evangelizes while serving the poor in her community and the poor in spirit nationally.

POWER SISTERS | 129

> *"I think that the Holy Spirit has great plans, not only for the Church in the United States but for the whole world. We just have to get out of the way and be the hands and feet and allow the Lord to touch hearts."* –
> Sister Alicia Torres

CHAPTER CHALLENGE

FAITH CHALLENGE

- Learn more about the Catholic church's three-year National Eucharistic Revival, aimed to inspire, educate, and unite the faithful in a more intimate relationship with Jesus in the Eucharist. Information can be found at their official website:

Consider participating in St. Ignatius' Spiritual Exercises. The Hallow app offers one with Fr. Timothy Gallagher that lasts twenty-eight days.

WORKS CHALLENGE

- Support the Laboure Society, a non-profit group dedicated to eliminating the educational debt of Roman Catholic religious candidates. Often, debt has kept some from answering God's call. Sister Alicia was one of their clients.

130 | SR. ALICIA TORRES

CHAPTER 11

SISTER MADONNA BUDER
POWER IRON NUN

> *"If I don't use the gifts God has given, I am not honoring my Creator."* – Sister Madonna Buder

Growing up in St. Louis with two brothers, Sr. Madonna Buder never played with dolls or did many stereotypical things girls from her generation did. She enjoyed the outdoors. She loved animals and, like many young children, loved dogs and horses.

Her cocker spaniel, Winkie, came as a gift on her twelfth birthday at a time when she really needed a friend after changing schools. Her love for riding horses would eventually evolve into a passion for riding a bicycle a few years later, but not until a priest introduced her to distance running at the age of forty-seven.

She took that first run on a beach appropriately on April 1 and quickly became a self-described fool for Christ. Five weeks later, she entered her first race. When she heard from her mother that one of her brothers was heading toward a divorce due to his alcoholism, she signed up for an 8.2 mile run.

Typically, new distance runners sign up for a 5K (3.1 miles) or 10K (6.2 miles) and then build up mileage, but Sister Madonna was not typical. She signed up for the longer distance, hoping the Lord would accept her willingness to endure hardship and transfer her strength to her brother. Although her race did not prevent her brother's eventual divorce, she did take some solace in that he beat his alcohol addiction. Years later, he remarried, and his wife did not drink.

Once she started competitively running, Sister Madonna rediscovered her adventurous spirit, which she had muted since entering the Sisters of the Good Shepherd and taking vows of poverty, chastity, obedience, and zeal. The latter vow drew her to the order since she had a zeal for the salvation of souls and adventures in life.

After increasing her training mileage, Sister Madonna ran the prestigious Boston Marathon multiple times within just a few years of picking up running; she then combined her childhood love for swimming with cycling and running to start competing in triathlons.

One could say the rest is history as she quickly started setting new age group records for women in their 50s, 60s, 70s, and 80s for Ironman distance triathlons. Her reputation as a top competitor in these races that cover nearly 150 miles (140.6 to be exact) earned her the nickname "Iron Nun."

To better understand this Iron Nun, it is worth exploring her journey before and after she accepted the call to her religious vocation. Like her training and racing, her journey had its share of challenges and victories.

Her mother endured a July heatwave that brought temperatures as high as 105 degrees to the St. Louis area to bring her daughter into the world, and that may explain some of the success Sister Madonna has had racing in the heat. After this hot start, Sister Madonna enjoyed a childhood with devoted parents and a special bond with her paternal grandfather. Ironically, that grandfather was hoping for a grandson to carry on the name since the Buder family had a strong reputation in the area as benefactors to Washington University, the opera, and some Mississippi riverfront landmarks.

Shortly after her birth, her paternal grandmother died suddenly, leaving her grandfather bedridden with grief. As a non-believer, he had no faith to lean on for hope. When he eventually formed a special bond with his new granddaughter, he not only arose but lived for another twenty-four years leading small adventures with his "little queen," as he nicknamed Madonna.

One family adventure almost ended tragically. When Sister Madonna was nine, she accompanied her parents and younger brother, the coveted male namesake, on a sailboat during a family vacation near Lake Michigan.

A sudden storm capsized their boat, and the little queen was pinned under the boat. She had been a strong swimmer since first learning at age two, so she decided to escape by holding her breath and diving down. After her mom pulled her brother out of a similar predicament while she prayed, the Coast Guard rescued the family. Prayers answered.

The rest of her childhood was less traumatic, but her prayers for a little sister were never answered. So, she resorted to dressing up her youngest of three brothers on occasion in her old clothes and found her solace in animals. The previously mentioned cocker spaniel her mother gave her for her twelfth birthday served as a companion on her outdoor adventures, and later, she became an accomplished equestrian.

When she turned twelve, her parents enrolled her in a school run by the Sisters of the Visitation, and although her mother and maternal grandmother had attended there, it initially felt like a dungeon to her. Eventually, the nuns at Visitation Academy made a positive impression on her despite the limited play time she had there compared to her previous school. She began to enjoy the chanting during vespers and incense at Benediction. The nuns even charmed her out of her stage fright, casting her as the lead female role in her eighth-grade play.

Her acting continued through high school, and she landed the lead role her senior year. At age fourteen, she already knew she wanted to be a religious sister, but she also enjoyed dating. She even met a medical school student at an equestrian event. Although they only went on one formal date, she was impressed by his sense of service to others.

That medical student, Tom Dooley, would go on to serve as a doctor in Vietnam as a Navy officer and a long-time humanitarian. He battled against disease and communism but would lose his personal battle with cancer, succumbing at the early age of thirty-four. His statue resides near the University of Notre Dame's grotto, a gift from the alumni of St. Louis.

In college at Washington University in St. Louis, Sister Madonna continued dating, and many described her as a social butterfly. Her equestrian competing ended abruptly when her horse died suddenly, and she felt the nudge to divest of worldly attachments. Around the same time, after seeing a passion play with her family, she was in tears thinking about the sacrifice and love Jesus showed by dying on the cross for us. She knew then she had to answer the call she heard years earlier.

> *"There is no greater love than to give one's life for another."* –John 15:13

While teaching first graders and continuing to act in theater, she discerned between joining the Sisters of the Visitation and the Sisters of the Good Shepherd. Both orders were semi-cloistered, which surprisingly did not dissuade the social butterfly. She appreciated the education and example of the Sisters of the Visitation. Their mission mirrored Mary's commitment to carry Jesus to others as she did when she visited her cousin Elizabeth while pregnant with John the Baptist. Ultimately, she felt the pull to the Sisters of the Good Shepherd and that zeal to save souls.

Her mother supported her decision, but her grandfather and dad, who was expecting an engagement to a young Marine she had recently dated, did not. A few days prior, her dad played tennis with her as his way of saying goodbye since he could not bear accompanying her to the convent for her final drop-off. Her brothers also struggled with the reality they could only see their sister once a month. Despite the lack of support, she entered the order as a postulant three weeks after playing the lead role of Grazia in *Death Takes a Holiday*. A beautiful note from her mother included, "I am most thankful to our Lord for choosing you as His own."

A few months after entering, her family, including her dad, visited her, showing their support for her decision. Since her grandfather did not join, she asked God for a sign before she made the next step to become a novice and receive her habit. She left the convent to visit her grandfather with permission and received her sign. As they sat down for snacks, the old man who spent the first eighty-three years of his life without faith made the sign of the cross and said the blessing over the food. Soon, he came to the convent, and a priest baptized him. Within weeks, he received the sacrament of the sick and died peacefully, knowing that his little queen would spend her life as a bride to his Lord.

Sister Madonna completed her journey toward her final vows, grateful for the blessings of her entire family, and jumped at a chance to spend some time at the Orders Mother House in Angers, France. It marked her second trip to Europe, and the future globetrotting nun relished the return to her mother's home country before returning to St. Louis to take her final vows.

In St. Louis, she taught high school classes and served as a group mother to young girls, and over the next few years, she would serve in similar roles in Kansas City, Phoenix, and San Francisco. The globetrotting continued when she was assigned as a family counselor in Spokane, Washinton, after graduating from Arizona State University with a master's in counseling and educational counseling. Wearing the habit pictured at the beginning of the chapter, the tall nun stood out on campus.

As a family counselor, Sister Madonna found herself in tears after some sessions as she struggled with the pain she heard. A friend recommended finding a hobby as an outlet, and she soon added photography. She used her hobby to create books from her photos to share God's message about life, death, and resurrection.

Following the 1965 Vatican II decree on the renewal of religious life (Perfectae Caritatis), sweeping changes came to religious communities. The council sought to promote the renewal of each religious institute through the members studying the original vision of their founder or foundress. Sister Madonna took liberty in the new guidance to join a new order called Sisters for Christian Community and began her life-long mission of counseling women in prison.

> *"Sorry, I can't talk any longer now; I have to go to jail."*
> – Sister Madonna

With her prison work, Sister Madonna rediscovered her zeal for souls. She found that women in jail were either hungry for God or could not care less about Him. Those seeking to amend their ways and rekindle their faith were incredibly grateful for the deep discussions they shared with her during her frequent visits. Her work was transformational, and she ran into former prisoners around Spokane on multiple occasions. One jailed for drugs shared, "I can't tell you how much you helped me while I was there. I've been clean ever since."

Connecting her hobbies to her Catholic faith was extremely important to Sister Madonna. As she started running, she discovered prayer and fitness blended well together. She also discovered her athletic prowess and longevity came naturally to her since her dad had been a champion oarsman and played handball regularly even after he turned seventy.

> *"I was running on faith, and I prayed while I ran."*
> – Sister Madonna

Knowing little about running, Sister Madonna did not properly train for that first 8.2-mile race, but she did finish. After a few marathons, which, as previously mentioned, included the famous Boston Marathon, which requires challenging qualifying times, Sister Madonna turned to triathlons and soon was doing full-distance Ironman races. She met some failures but kept the faith to become a champion.

> *"The only failure is not to try because your effort in itself is a success."* – Sister Madonna

In her first Ironman race in Kona, Hawaii, she did not even make the cutoff time for the first event, the 2.4-mile swim. Instead of wallowing in her disappointment, she used the opportunity to encourage a priest struggling to finish the second event, cycling 112 miles under the required time. He made the biking cutoff and completed the marathon run of 26.2 miles in time.

Sr. Madonna overcame many injuries and challenges throughout her four decades of competing in triathlons. Some of her injuries included:

- A fractured elbow after a biking accident
- A broken hip and femur
- Two broken toes the night before a race

These injuries do not include the stomach aches, dehydration, and sheer exhaustion of competing in these grueling distance races.

Through it all, Sister Madonna never lost her sense of caring for others and spreading the message of faith. In addition to her ongoing prison ministry, she often leads the competitors in prayer before the race. She also raises money for charity when she competes. Just as she helped the struggling priest finish the bike event, she has inspired athletes of all ages.

> "Don't waste time trying to deny or disguise your age; embrace those wrinkles; you earned them."
> – Sister Madonna

At the age of 93, Sister Madonna is still racing! She has competed in nearly four hundred triathlons, including about 50 Ironman-distance races. In 2006, she became the oldest person to finish an Ironman triathlon and set several age-group records. Sr. Madonna began to receive national attention for her accomplishments and published her autobiography in 2010 entitled *The Grace to Race-- The Wisdom and Inspiration of the 80-Year-Old World Champion Triathlete*.

> *"You're never too old to learn, so you're never too old to tri" (purposely spelled this way).*
> – Sister Madonna

Popular with triathletes and Catholics alike, in the book, the Iron Nun shared stories that infused her competitions and faith. With her travels all over the world to compete, she shared how the "angels" who came to help her often resembled biblical figures.

- A carpenter by trade who determined the cause of her broken down car on the way to church reminded her of Jesus' father on earth, St. Joseph.
- A barefoot, hairy-chested, shirtless bearded man who drove 2 hours to return her wallet after she left it at a race resembled St. John the Baptist.
- A group of drunk fishermen who pulled up in a truck when she ran out of gas and, by the grace of God, returned safely with gas for her reminded her of the first pope and fisherman, St. Peter.

Her fame grew even more when Nike featured her as the first athlete in their "Unlimited Youth" advertising campaign, which aired during the 2016 Olympics. She humbly shared, "I do not understand how a little old lady can inspire anybody. But I do not have to understand. I just want to fulfill God's will, and if God's putting me out there to encourage others as they advance in years, I accept it."

Even with all the fame and forty years of competing as a triathlete, Sister Madonna's primary mission as a religious sister for seventy years continues to be doing God's will and saving souls.

> *"Take care of your body as if you are going to live forever; take care of your soul as if you are going to die tomorrow."* – Saint Augustine

Sister Madonna Bruder continues to win hearts and souls as she competes around the world. As she approaches the finish line of this life, the little queen-turned-Iron Nun continues to inspire and shares her seven "D" steps for success:

- Dream
- Desire
- Dedication
- Discipline
- Determination
- Dare
- Do it!

Those steps in order can help one successfully achieve any goal. Sister Madonna hopes one of those goals is to do God's will, even if it is unique at any age.

> *"Dream what you want to do, then you can desire it. Once you desire it, start putting in the discipline."*
> –Sister Madonna Bruder

CHAPTER CHALLENGE

FAITH CHALLENGE

- Learn the Corporal and Spiritual works of mercy:

  CORPORAL WORKS OF MERCY
  - feed the hungry
  - give drink to the thirsty
  - give alms to the poor
  - shelter the homeless
  - visit the sick
  - visit the imprisoned
  - bury the dead

  SPIRITUAL WORKS OF MERCY
  - instruct the ignorant
  - counsel the doubtful
  - admonish the sinner
  - forgive injuries
  - comfort the sorrowful
  - bear wrongs patiently
  - pray for the living and the dead

WORKS CHALLENGE

- Consider supporting a prison ministry or regularly practicing one of the works of mercy.

- If you are not exercising regularly, consider starting and becoming fit for our King, God in heaven. If you exercise outdoors that is also a way to pray and spend time with God because it is His creation.

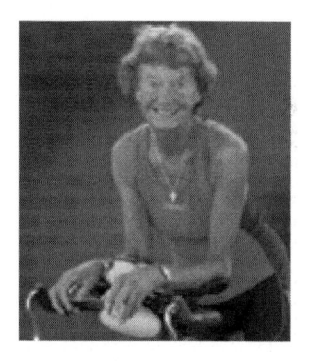

CHAPTER 12

SISTER MIRIAM JAMES HEIDLAND
POWER HITTER, AUTHOR, AND PODCASTER

> *"We all want to be sought after, found, and held by the perfect father, who is God."* –Sr. Mariam James

As a young girl raised in Woodland, Washington, Sharon Heidland, who would become Sister Mariam James, had a close relationship with her mother. As she played, she dreamed of being a princess and pictured herself looking like her mother as an adult.

When she was seven, Sharon was browsing through a family photo album and enjoying pictures of family trips and even one of her brothers tied to a teeter-totter, but she noticed something was missing. Not realizing the answer to her next question would change her innocent vision of her future, she asked, "Mom, how come there aren't any pictures of you pregnant with me?"

After a long silence, her mother explained how she and her father had adopted her as a baby since they couldn't conceive a child. Her birth parents were seventeen-year-olds who wanted the best for their child despite an unplanned pregnancy and not having the means to care for a newborn.

Part of Sharon's heart felt numb that day. How does a young girl comprehend that the origin of her very existence was a "mistake" in some people's definition? Encouraged by her mother not to tell others, Sharon felt like she had this dark secret that needed to be hidden.

As she grew older and prayed more, Sharon realized that God does not make mistakes. Her birth had a purpose; despite some detours along her journey, she found her calling and the way.

> *"I did not want to be ordinary... I wanted to do something great with my life."* –Sr. Mariam James

Her parents raised her and her brother Catholic, ensuring they all went to Mass every Sunday and received the proper training for the sacraments. Although it would take Sharon time to realize the foundation of her faith was God's caring love and not a list of duties, obligations, and prohibitions, the seeds of her faith were planted.

Her relationship with her mother eventually grew even stronger as she realized the bond between a mother and child was not limited by shared genetics. Their relationship was built on the love they showed for each other, just as our relationship with our heavenly Father grows through our love for Him.

When she was turning fifteen, Sharon wanted a specific wristwatch. Her mother had already picked out a watch for her, but as a loving mother, she agreed to let her teen pick out her own. At the mall store, Sharon picked among over forty watches, the very same one her mom had already gotten for her.

Their loving bond was evident, and despite not sharing genetics, her mother knew what was best for her. The watch foreshadowed an even greater gift her mother would give her-- the power of intercessory prayers.

> *"The relationships we have on earth are supposed to reflect the deep love and care God has for us."*
> – Sr. Mariam James

As a tall, lanky teen, Sharon started playing volleyball in middle school and excelled. Her parents supported her new passion and let her join a club team in high school. Her height and natural skills were soon noticed.

While playing for her club team at a national tournament in Las Vegas, colleges scouted her. During her senior year in high school, she signed a full scholarship to play for the University of Nevada-Reno. Yet, her success on the volleyball court was masking an interior struggle.

Psychologists report that one in four girls will be sexually abused by the time they are eighteen. Sexual abuse can lead the victim to shame, guilt, depression, promiscuity, and even substance abuse to deal with the pain she feels inside. Sister Mariam James should know. She was such a victim.

She shared the following in her book, *Loved As I Am*:

"I remember sitting by the window one day as a girl after a certain instance of abuse. I had been taken advantage of for the abuser's gratification and cast aside when it was over. I felt completely emptied by the abuse and subsequent disorder that shattered my interior life and innocence. As I sat there and stared at my socks, I was heartbroken and confused, feeling completely stripped of anything good, true, or beautiful. After the abuse, something within me died."

POWER SISTERS | 145

Those same psychologists who share the sad fact that twenty-five percent of girls will be abused also know the victim's mental suffering continues well after the incidents of abuse. Healing can only start when the victim shares her story and stops blaming herself.

Sister Mariam did not tell anyone what happened during those instances of violation, so she alone carried the pain and scars-hurting herself and others along the way. Her relationship with her parents became strained, and understandably, her faith suffered. How could a loving God let this happen? Why would He hand anyone such a difficult cross to carry? God looked very different through the broken lens of abuse.

> *"Anyone who treats a person as the means to an end does violence to the very essence of the other... We should never treat a person as a means to an end."*
> –Saint John Paul II

Sister Mariam carried her cross with her to college, and even while playing D1 volleyball, she turned to drinking and promiscuity to mask the pain. While ingesting a steady diet of MTV, fashion magazines, and partying, she realized she was broken inside while trying to appear as perfect as possible to others. Her exterior was a facade that hid her deep pain and addiction to alcohol and sex. She stopped going to Mass and did whatever she wanted.

When her parents visited her at college, they could see that she had lost her way by the way she was living. They were displeased at how she was living and who she was dating and cut her off financially in hopes she would stop her rebellious and sinful ways.

After one such trip, her dad confided in her mom just before they fell asleep that he was so disappointed in Sharon. Her mother leaped out of bed and went to the prayer room in their home and fervently prayed that their daughter, who was eight hundred miles away living in addiction and open mortal sin, would become a nun!

A religious vocation was so far from Sharon's plans. She was majoring in speech communications, and when not focused on volleyball or partying, she dreamt of working someday for ESPN or a news network.

During her junior year, a knee injury requiring surgery would throw her volleyball season and her plans for a loop. After surgery, Sharon was on crutches and could not move without pain. Thanks to the help of a fantastic friend and athletic trainer, she steadily improved and saw the power of kindness.

During the rehabilitation, she had time to reflect on her life and her parents' advice. Despite doing what she thought was the typical path of a college student: dating, partying, and playing sports, she was unhappy.

As she wrote in her book, she soon realized she was looking in the wrong place for happiness. She shared, "OK, I have a boyfriend who's really good-looking. I've got a full scholarship. I have decent grades, school's never hard, and I do pretty much whatever I want. So why am I so unhappy?"

> *"Addictions are usually a feeble attempt to escape emotional pain in our lives."* – Sr. Mariam James

Soon after recovering from her knee injury, Sister Mariam started to rekindle her faith and change her ways. After graduating and moving back to Washington, she found help from a Catholic priest, Fr. Santan Pinto, who guided her along her faith journey.

POWER SISTERS | 147

> "God is in every person's life. Even if a person's life has been a disaster or destroyed by vices, drugs, or anything else -- God is in this person's life."
> –Pope Francis

Fr. Pinto, originally from India, has his own story. He worked for some time with Mother Teresa, who taught him to recognize Jesus in the poor. Mother Teresa once said to him: "Remember, Father, that it is the humility of God that made you a priest. Now, never forget that!"

He shared some of the lies that Satan seeks to plant in believers' hearts, including:

- We are fatherless and all alone.
- God sucks the fun out of everything.
- True freedom exists in doing what we want.

> "Whenever a person turns to the Lord, the veil is removed... And where the spirit of the Lord is, there is freedom."
> –2 Corinthians 3:16-17

True freedom is identifying what is truly good and then choosing the good rather than choosing sin. When one becomes addicted to something, they become a slave to those addictions and loses that freedom.

After graduation, she reconnected with Father Santan Pinto, who had been introduced to her by her parents during her freshman year of college. Father Pinto, who founded the Society of Our Lady of the Most Holy Trinity Ministries, encouraged her to visit a mission in New Mexico, and she found her calling.

Although she thought there was no way she was cut out to be a missionary, she trusted him. The mission didn't have any television, radio, or Wi-Fi. There wasn't much to distract her, so she had a lot of time to be silent. The hopeful television reporter was without any media for a few weeks.

In a moment of radical conversion, she heard Jesus calling her to be his bride. Even though her life was a train wreck, it was there in the silence of the mission that she heard Jesus Christ calling her. A ray of grace just pierced her soul, and she knew in an instant her call to a religious life.

After three years of training in Rome, Sister Mariam took her final vows. As a member of the Society of Our Lady of the Most Holy Trinity, she earned her master's degree in theology from the Augustine Institute. She took courses at the Theology of the Body Institute.

Her first assignment landed her in Dunseith, N.D., a small town near the Canadian border where she coached the high-school volleyball team. She was then sent to Seattle, and as a member of the Society of Our Lady of the Most Holy Trinity (S.O.L.T), she lived at a parish. Her schedule was filled with prayer time and teaching middle-school P.E. and music, but she also found time for volleyball.

She drove 20 miles to coach volleyball at a local Catholic high school, Archbishop Murphy and played locally for a club team. She never really set out to be a coach, but she felt the call was divinely inspired.

Even after she entered the religious life, Sister Mariam needed further healing to overcome some of the demons of her past. Her father's sudden death a few years after she entered the S.O.L.T. order triggered some pain she experienced as a child.

POWER SISTERS | 149

Why had God taken him away so soon and so suddenly? Fortunately, she received the professional help she needed and could return to her order after a short hiatus. She returned with an even stronger sense of gratitude for her parents, who raised her with the foundation of the Catholic Church and showed her the tough love she needed in college. She credited both as critical factors in her recovery.

> "When we have wounds of abandonment and rejection, the Evil One uses them as a conduit to whisper the lies that no one loves us, and no one will be there for us or care for us. When these wounds go unhealed, our lives become dysfunctional." –Sister Mariam in *Loved As I Am*

She still loves sports and often talks about different sporting events or competitions. She feels sports can be an excellent path to virtue, learning, and self-sacrifice. Her hours of digging, setting, and spiking on the volleyball court transformed into praying, reading, and teaching. All require practice and practicing what you preach as a religious sister.

> "I believe that the most powerful gospel we will ever preach is how we live our daily lives."
> –Sr. Mariam James

As she travels around, she often speaks to young adults on the *Theology of the Body*, healing in Jesus, pop culture, beauty, and the transforming power of authentic love. Her background as a college athlete and survivor of childhood abuse provides engaging personal stories demonstrating how the power of God's love can heal and the beauty of Church teachings. That teaching in *Theology of the Body* emphasizes that we are made in the image and likeness of God, and true happiness comes in using our bodies as designed by God to love and serve him. She strives to instill the power of God's love in the hearts of those to whom she speaks.

> *"Seek excellence in your sport and give yourself fully at practices and at games. Learn the lessons God is trying to teach you in your daily life and have fun. But always remember that sports are not the final goal of our lives. It's very important to have balance in life. Many times, we worship at the altar of sports rather than God. Sports will pass away; God never will."* –Sr. Mariam James

She also uses the example of her biological parents to advocate for the protection of unborn children. Despite the pain she felt when she found out she was adopted, she grew grateful for the sacrifice her teenage parents made for her. Her mother's choice to carry her for nine months and give her up for adoption inspires her faith and her audience. Little did that teenage mother know she was carrying a future power sister.

Learn more at:
Theology of the Body for Teens

POWER SISTERS | 151

As she works with Catholic teens, Sister Mariam sees the challenges facing them today, with the media inundating them with lies about what brings happiness. She sees their tremendous desire for happiness and purpose in life. She sees deep questions of what it means to love God, oneself, and other people. Those who seek God and want to be a witness in the world inspire her.

As a religious sister, her habit is a visible sign of her commitment to Jesus, and when people meet her in public, they often ask for prayers or to talk. Some will tell her their deepest secrets, and some will say awkward things, but one thing is for sure: she never goes out unnoticed ever again.

Even as a beautiful and happy woman, Sister Mariam admits sometimes, when she looks in the mirror, she does not find the reflection too pleasant. Despite her success as an athlete, coach, and now podcaster, she needs God to remind her He made her in His beautiful image and likeness.

One morning, she was feeling down, and when she arrived at Mass, she plopped into the pew for an hour of self-pity and reluctant worship. Afterward, she genuflected and made her way to the back of the church. She was greeted by an older woman with her five-year-old granddaughter. As Sister Mariam bent down to greet the young girl, she looked up at her with eyes of wonder and said, "You look like a princess."

The young woman from Washington needed the reminder from a child about the true definition of a princess -- a daughter of a King. She was not the victim of someone's lustful sins or the sum of her failures. In her veil, Sister Mariam was the perfect definition of a princess. Like her mother, she was sharing the beauty and wonder of her Catholic faith with others since God's love conquered all her shortcomings. Her childhood dream had come true.

This princess-looking sister does not sit on a throne or even let the dust settle under her feet. Sr. Miriam James Heidland, SOLT, has become a popular Catholic speaker, co-host of the *Abiding Together* podcast, and the author of the bestselling books *Loved as I Am, Behold,* and *Restore.* She also leads healing retreats at the John Paul II Healing Center.

On the *Abiding Together* podcast, she teams up with her friends Heather Khym and Michelle Benzinger to provide a place of connection, rest, and encouragement for women on the journey of living out their passion and purpose in Jesus Christ. Her books provide genuine and relatable details about her faith journey, and as she shares this chapter, like an ice cream sample, offers just a small portion of her amazing story and insights.

CHAPTER CHALLENGE

FAITH CHALLENGE

- Discover the healing power of a thorough confession and start by learning the Act of Contrition.

  O my God, I am heartily sorry for having offended Thee, and I detest all my sins because of Thy just punishments, but most of all, because they offend Thee, my God, Who are all-good and deserving of all my love. I firmly resolve, with the help of Thy grace, to sin no more and to avoid in the near occasion of sin. Amen.

- Read or listen to Sr. Mariam's books and podcasts.

WORKS CHALLENGE

- Volunteer or support the Franciscan Peacemakers who provide a pathway to healing for women who have been sexually exploited. They offer housing, employment, and a healing network of support to women while advocating to end human sex trafficking. Women survivors earn a living wage through their social enterprise, gain job experience, and engage in meaningful employment handcrafting bath, body, and home goods. These products nurture peace and goodness in the lives of women survivors and advocate for an end to sexual exploitation. Scan the QR code to see their items.

CHAPTER 13
WRAP UP

Please end with the Serran Prayer for Vocations.

O God, Who wills not the death of a sinner, but instead that he be converted and live, grant we beseech You through the intercession of the Blessed Mary, ever Virgin, Saint Joseph, her spouse, Saint Junipero Serra, and all the saints, an increase of laborers for your Church, fellow laborers with Christ to spend and consume themselves for souls, through the same Jesus Christ, Your Son, Who lives and reigns with You, in the unity of the Holy Spirit, God forever and ever. Amen.

After researching and interviewing these religious sisters, a few themes consistently repeat in their lives:

1. Although some answered the call to their religious vocation later in life, all felt a draw as teenagers.
2. Regular prayer, scripture reading, and time before the Eucharist gave them strength and direction.
3. They believe in science and protecting life from conception to natural death.
4. They love their vocation and the people they have been called to serve.
5. They find strength from their fellow sisters and the example set by Mary.

> *"I felt a special relationship with the virgin Mary. What more powerful intermediary can we have than the Blessed Mother?"* –Sister Madonna Bruder

Sister Mary Kenneth Keller and Sr. Maureen McGuire are two other religious sisters worthy of the title of power sisters. A brief overview will have to do since there is limited information about their early lives.

Sister Keller was the first person (man or woman) to receive a PhD. in computer science. In the 1960s, this Catholic nun wrote the computer language BASIC, which essentially opened the floodgates for computer programming. She founded the computer science department at Clarke University and led it for twenty years. Little is known of her life before she joined the Sisters of Charity of the Blessed Virgin Mary in 1932. She passed away in 1985, at seventy-one, leaving a legacy as a computer science pioneer.

Sister Maureen served as a senior executive at Ascension Health for nearly two decades as a Senior Vice President and then Executive Vice President and Chief Mission Integration Officer. She took her vows as a Daughter of Charity in 1967 and, after a master's degree in social work from Temple University, did social work. She started one of the nation's first transitional housing programs for homeless women and children affected by HIV/AIDS before joining the healthcare network. One colleague called her a "humble Holy Spirit-filled dynamo" with an incredible way of connecting with people.

Sister Maureen McGuire shared that God put the mission and healthcare work in her heart, and she just followed His call-- another consistent theme for all these power sisters.

References and Notes

Unless otherwise noted, all Bible quotes are from bible.usccb.org

"Abbey of Regina Laudis: Mother Dolores Hart." Abbey of Regina Laudis, https://abbeyofreginalaudis.org/community-mdh.html.

"About Us | Ascension." About | Ascension, https://about.ascension.org/about-us.

Agency, Catholic News. "Meet the Navy Veteran Who Became a Sister of Life: 'My Heart Was Made For.'" Denver Catholic, Denver Catholic, 11 Nov. 2021, https://denvercatholic.org/meet-the-navy-veteran-who-became-a-sister-of-life-my-heart-was-made-for-something-more/.

Alicia. "Who Is Poor, Anyway? - FOCUS." FOCUS, https://www.facebook.com/focuscatholic/, 2 Mar. 2022, https://focusequip.org/who-is-poor-anyway/.

"Antona Ebo, F.S.M.: 1924-2017 : SLU." Saint Louis University | SLU.Edu : SLU, https://www.slu.edu/news/2017/november/sister-antona-ebo-obit.php.

Arroyo, Raymond. Mother Angelica. Image, 2007.

Batura, Paul. "Elvis Presley, Dolores Hart, The Bible and The Actress Who Became a Nun - Daily Citizen." Daily Citizen, 8 Nov. 2022, https://dailycitizen.focusonthefamily.com/elvis-presley-dolores-hart-the-bible-and-the-actress-who-became-a-nun/.

Buder, Sister Madonna, and Karin Evans. The Grace to Race. Simon and Schuster, 2010.

Contributors to Wikimedia projects. "Madonna Buder - Wikipedia." Wikipedia, the Free Encyclopedia, Wikimedia Foundation, Inc., 9 Apr. 2006, https://en.wikipedia.org/wiki/Madonna_Buder.

"Dr. M. Therese Antone RSM | Salve Regina University." Salve Regina University - Learn, Lead, Make a Difference. | Salve Regina University, https://salve.edu/users/dr-m-therese-antone-rsm.

"EWTN Global Catholic Television Network: Catholic News, TV, Radio | EWTN." EWTN Global Catholic Television Network, https://www.ewtn.com/motherangelica/.

"Fit Chicks: The Iron Nun, Sister Madonna Buder - Paste Magazine." Paste Magazine, https://www.facebook.com/PasteMagazine, https://www.pastemagazine.com/health/fitness/fit-chicks-the-iron-nun-sister-madonna-buder/.

Garrett, Sister Josephine. "Black Catholics Need to Tell Their Stories." Our Sunday Visitor, https://www.facebook.com/OurSundayVisitor, 5 Feb. 2021, https://www.oursundayvisitor.com/black-catholics-need-to-tell-their-stories/.

Heidland, Miriam James. Loved as I Am. Ave Maria Press, 2014.

"I Won the Cooking Competition 'Chopped.' But as a Catholic Sister, My Ministry Focuses on a Deeper Hunger. | America Magazine." America Magazine, 16 Sept. 2021, https://www.americamagazine.org/faith/2021/09/16/chopped-winner-catholic-service-eucharist-241383.

Institute. 2021 GIVEN Forum - Sister DeDe Byrne - Sister, Soldier, Surgeon. YouTube, 12 Nov. 2021, https://www.youtube.com/watch?v=hXBus9toXnk.

"Sister Dede Answers the Call - Georgetown Today." Georgetown Today, https://www.facebook.com/georgetownalumni, 16 Oct. 2016, https://today.advancement.georgetown.edu/health-magazine/2016/sister-dede-byrne/.

"Meet the 'nun with the Gun' Honored at the 2019 White Mass." Angelus News - Multimedia Catholic News, https://www.facebook.com/AngelusNews/, 15 Oct. 2019, https://angelusnews.com/local/la-catholics/meet-the-nun-with-the-gun-honored-at-the-white-mass/.

Mother Angelica Live Classic - 1997-11-04 - How To Read The Bible. YouTube, 9 Apr. 2015, https://www.youtube.com/watch?v=vCpGc2fWle4.

Mother Teresa: No Greater Love. Castletown Media, 2022.

"Office of the Chancellor | Salve Regina University." Salve Regina University - Learn, Lead, Make a Difference. | Salve Regina University, https://www.salve.edu/office-of-chancellor.

Rose, Jordan. "Vocation Story: Sr. Maris Stella - Sisters of Life." Sisters of Life, 1 Jan. 2019, https://sistersoflife.org/2019/01/01/vocation-story-sms/.

"Selma March." Encyclopedia Britannica, Encyclopedia Britannica, https://www.britannica.com/event/Selma-March.

"Sr. Maureen McGuire, DC, Shaped, Strengthened Catholic Health Care through Formation of Laity." Www.Chausa.Org, https://www.chausa.org/publications/catholic-health-world/archive/article/july-1-2022/sr.-maureen-mcguire-dc-shaped-strengthened-catholic-health-care-through-formation-of-laity

"St. Teresa Benedicta of the Cross (Edith Stein) - Boston Carmel." Boston Carmel, https://carmelitesofboston.org/history/our-carmelite-saints/st-teresa-benedicta-of-the-cross-edith-stein/.

Teresa, Mother. A Simple Path. Ballantine Books, 1995.

Teresa, Mother, and Brian Kolodiejchuk. Mother Teresa: Come Be My Light: image, 2009.

"That Beautiful Black Nun: Sister Antona Ebo – OperationalizeBeauty." OperationalizeBeauty, https://www.facebook.com/WordPresscom, 10 Mar. 2016, https://operationalizebeauty.com/2016/03/10/that-beautiful-black-nun-sister-antona-ebo/.

"'The Eucharist Is My Strength': The Story of Sr Alicia Torres - Vatican News." News from the Vatican - News about the Church - Vatican News, 15 June 2022, https://www.vaticannews.va/en/church/news/2022-06/sisters-project-eucharist-alicia-torres.html.

The New York Times. "Breaking Bread: Dominique Dawes and Mother Angelica - NYTimes.Com." The New York Times - Breaking News, US News, World News and Videos, 17 Aug. 2016, https://www.nytimes.com/interactive/projects/cp/obituaries/archives/dominique-dawes-mother-angelica.

"The Unsung Women of Science - Part 3." TechJuice, http://facebook.com/techjuicepk, 27 Sept. 2019, https://www.techjuice.pk/sister-mary-kenneth-keller/.

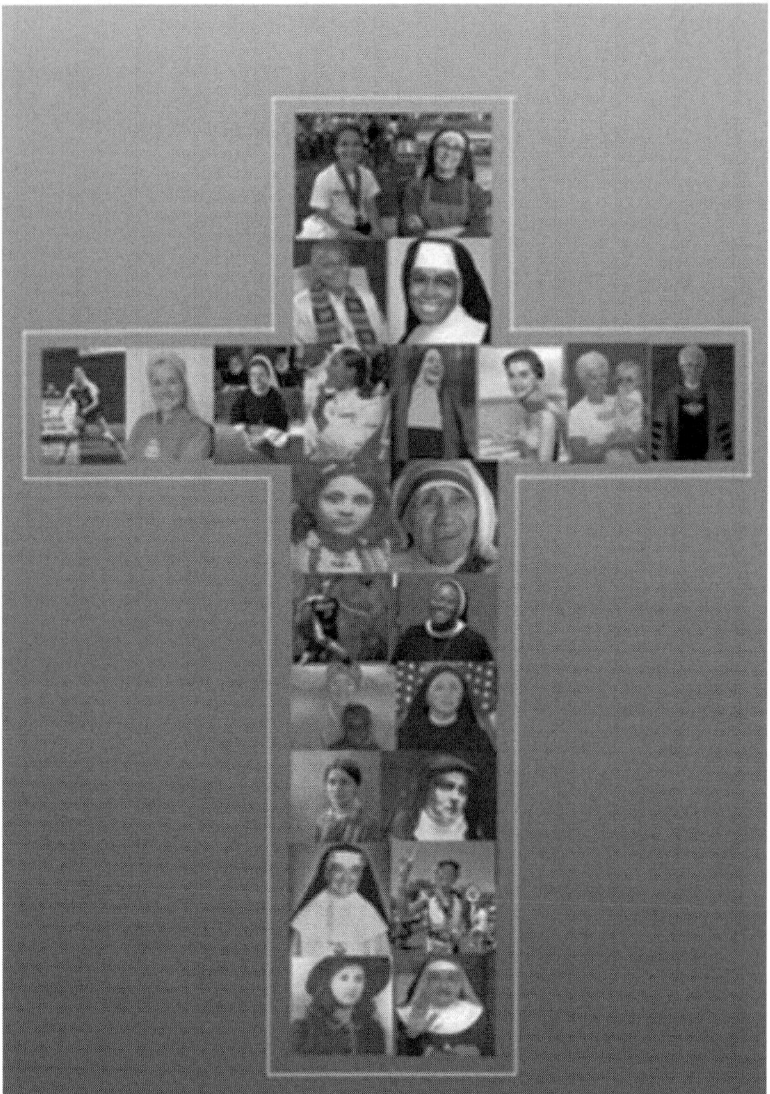

About the Author

Greg is the proud father of five children and is a graduate of the University of Notre Dame with a master's degree from Cornell University. As an Army officer, he completed the demanding Ranger school and led his scout platoon on a successful deployment in North Macedonia. During his assignment in Germany, he traveled much of Europe, including trips to Fatima and the Vatican for Christmas Mass with Saint John Paul II. Since leaving the military as a captain, he has worked in the airline and technology industries for over twenty years.

His books have been featured on EWTN radio and in various Catholic publications. He founded **fromHeaven Books** after publishing his first book, *Mommying from Heaven,* honoring his late wife, Allison, who passed away shortly after the birth of their third child. Some of the priests featured in *Power Priests* supported him through that grieving process and faith journey. He is a Serra club member, ambassador for Guadalupe Radio Network, and a featured speaker at Catholic teen and vocational events.

Greg and his wife, MaryBeth, live in Flower Mound, Texas. He enjoys fitness and supporting veterans and teens, especially with their faith journey, emphasizing a strong mind, body, and soul. Along with writing, his interests include traveling, staying active, playing, and coaching various sports, and volunteering. He has sponsored pro-life dinners and talks by Chris Stefanick and Fr. Mike Schmitz.

Connect with him at fromHeaven Books:

Greg with his daughter, Beth, & Fr. Mike Schmitz

Made in the USA
Columbia, SC
09 February 2025